The Forensics of B2B Selling

The Forensics of B2B Selling

A Field Guide to Selling Success in the B2B Space

Neal Lappe

ISBN-13: 9781522933113
ISBN-10: 1522933115
Library of Congress Control Number: 2016900035
CreateSpace Independent Publishing Platform
North Charleston, South Carolina

Table of Contents

One

Introduction

How to become a better salesperson by reading this book...
This isn't necessarily a book you read cover-to-cover. It's more of a reference guide – a field manual – a group of articles you can review when you want to improve your performance in certain areas of sales.

The content of this book was assembled over the last few years as I experienced firsthand the B2B selling space. It's a combination of my participation in several sales training courses, reading many books about selling, and the actual experience selling solutions to clients in virtually all industries. It combines academic learning and practical experience.

I have read countless books about selling and credit a good amount of my personal success to a few books that I encourage you to read as well – if you haven't already. They are *The Challenger Sale* by Matthew Dixon and Brent Adamson, *Selling Excellence* by Jerry Acuff, *Spin Selling* by Neil Rackham, and *Fanatical Prospecting* by Jeb Blount. Each of these is based on extensively experienced selling or field studies of successful salespeople and sales organizations. In other words, the principles in these books are based on empirical data.

In addition to my academic learning, many years of experience selling in the B2B space have taught me what works and what doesn't. During this time, my firm also conducted proprietary research about what decision-makers value from salespeople. As a result, the digital marketing company I founded in 2004 has grown to be in the top 1% among over 1,000 peer firms from the worldwide network in which I belong. This sales experience and the associated success along with research inspired much of the content in this book.

I encourage you to scan through the Table of Contents and find the topics you want to learn first. Best of success in your sales development journey!

Two

Basic Marketing—Online and Offline

You can't sell anything until you have a qualified prospect that has a problem you can solve. This section is all about doing the right marketing to get the attention of your target market and qualified buyers.

HOW TO DEVELOP A SALES & MARKETING MACHINE

According to a leading global research firm, *"more than 67% percent of the buyer's buying journey is now done digitally, and 57% of the actual purchase decision is complete before a buyer even contacts a supplier"*... in other words, anonymous to the supplier. A second source of research data supports this finding..."*about 70% of the B2B buyer's journey is made anonymously in self-discovery mode with online content—not via direct marketing and sales interactions. This is just the opposite of a few years ago when 30% of the journey was marketing and 70% sales."*

The B2B buying process is mirroring the B2C process more and more—that is, buyers are empowered with so much information, they don't need the traditional sales channel to educate them. Instead, extensive online research, and conferring with their online and offline social networks are how they start the buying process. Consequently, your online assets (website, content, landing pages, blogs, social posts, etc.) must tell a more compelling story than your competitions. Otherwise, you may have lost an opportunity to make a customer for life. To the marketer, this feels a bit like being blindfolded while playing "hide and seek" with your buyers.

Smart marketers have found a way to connect with those buyers at the top end of the buying funnel and guide them through the buying process to ultimately do business with you—creating a sales machine that allows you to succeed in the "hide and seek" game with your target market.

The following are four important elements to create an effective sales and marketing system for your company...

1. ESTABLISH BUYER PERSONAS

How on earth can you connect and nurture your targeted buyer through the buying funnel if you don't know his or her pain points, value drivers, criteria for making decisions, etc.? Many businesses fail to understand their buyer's decision processes and what problems they can help them solve. This results in a lot of marketing investments that don't pay off.

Companies should invest in researching their buyer personas and establish a finite set of unique characteristics that describe how each type of buyer researches, behaves, and buys throughout the buying funnel process. Without this knowledge of your buyer, a business risks turning their sales and marketing efforts into "throwing spaghetti against the wall hoping something will stick".

Action: Invest time to research your buyer personas in order to identify a finite set, maybe 2-5, of unique buyer types (personalities) for your business.

2. DEVELOP & OFFER THE RIGHT CONTENT

In today's marketing world, the term "content marketing" is about as popular as the social media rage a few years ago. Why, because buyers go online to learn, research, compare, etc. and content is the key to their education. The content could be a blog post, whitepaper, video, or other form of delivering information online. But what if your content pales in comparison to that offered by your competitors? What if the content you develop and offer up doesn't really connect to your buyer's pain points, problems or unique demands? Then the time and money you invested in content marketing is sub-optimized.

The content you produce should be targeted to the personas you developed in #1 above, and it should address each of the unique stages in the buying funnel. The typical buying funnel stages include 1) research, 2) learn, 3) compare, and 4) purchase. Content—in whatever format is most appropriate for your buyer—should guide them through this buying funnel. The content that educates the buyer during the "learn" phase is different from the content that will help the buyer during the "compare" phase.

Action: Identify content themes for each of your buyer personas during the four stages of the buying process.

3. PROVIDE AUTOMATED MESSAGING IN A PROGRESSIVE WAY

A recent survey reported that less than 25% of current email campaigns were automatically triggered (see chart below). What this means is that few companies are using marketing automation to guide their buyers through the buying funnel. Think of a scenario in which a person comes to your website and downloads a piece of content they find valuable during their research process. A few days later, that person receives another piece of content from you that answers more of their questions. A week after that, the person receives information about how to evaluate the products or services he or she is researching. And then a week after that the person receives a discount offer for that product. You see where this is going –an automated way that helps the buyer progress through the buying funnel.

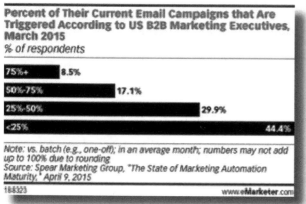

Percent of Their Current Email Campaigns that Are Triggered According to US B2B Marketing Executives, March 2015
% of respondents

75%+	8.5%
50%-75%	17.1%
25%-50%	29.9%
<25%	44.4%

Note: vs. batch (e.g., one-off); in an average month; numbers may not add up to 100% due to rounding
Source: Spear Marketing Group, "The State of Marketing Automation Maturity," April 9, 2015
188323 www.eMarketer.com

Marketing automation platforms like Hubspot, Marketo, and others can be programmed to assess buyer activities. These platforms send timely and unique messaging in line with where a buyer is at in the buying funnel. Setting up systems like this may be time-consuming, but think of the sales and marketing "machine" you will have in place once set up.

Action: Research marketing automation platforms and invest to establish a solid sales and marketing system for your company.

4. MEASURE ENGAGEMENT AND REACH OUT

Remember back in the day when you were contemplating your first kiss? Go for it too quickly and the other person might think you are too aggressive and be turned off. Act too slowly and the other person might lose patience and move on. Well, the same holds true for sales—go for the deal too soon and you might be "just another pushy salesperson"...fail to ask for the sale at the right time and your buyer might get frustrated and engage with a competitor.

Marketing automation systems like those mentioned in #3 above are able to "score" an individual based on his/her activity. Did the person open the email you sent to them? Did they go back to your website after reading the email? What did they do when they went back to your website? Did they go to a pricing page or some other page in your website that suggests a high level of interest? Knowing how interested your buyer is will help you gauge when to reach out.

Action: Track your buyer's activities and engage in the sales process only when they appear ready, or as I often refer to as – "sales qualified".

In today's online world, your buyers are checking you out without you knowing it. They are winning at the "hide and seek" game. Get to know them by researching their personas. Help your buyers come to the surface sooner by offering great content that appeals to their unique persona. Set up a system that nurtures them through the buying funnel, and then reach out when the time is right. Do these four things and you will have a very well-oiled sales and marketing machine.

HOW TO COMPETE SUCCESSFULLY - EXCELLING IN A COMPETITIVE MARKETPLACE

Charles Darwin said, "It is not the strongest species that survive, nor the most intelligent, but the ones most responsive to change". How this applies to you is determined by many factors. With the marketplace becoming ever more competitive and buyers' attitudes influenced by many elements, successful salespeople and businesses need to focus on three important factors to ensure they not only adapt and survive but excel.

Before digging into these three factors, let's establish a foundation for a successful enterprise. To succeed in the long run, a business must do three things consistently well...

- Create and acquire new customers by offering products/services of value to the marketplace
- Retain and grow existing customers by ensuring the "emotionomics" are in favor of the customer (more on "emotionomics" later)
- Evolve your product and service offerings so you remain relevant as your competitive marketplace evolves over time.

These elements are the foundation of any successful business over time. However, in an eternally intense competitive environment, these are "table stakes" as they say. To excel in a competitive environment, you must 1) decide who is best served by your products and services, 2) know your buyer's value drivers, and 3) deliver exceptional customer experiences.

WHO IS BEST SERVED BY YOUR PRODUCTS/SERVICES?

Your company does certain things well and other things not as well. The things you do well are considered your core competencies. These are things you are particularly good at and perhaps consider your competitive advantages. If you are not certain what your core competencies are you need to find out.

You can determine your core competencies in the following ways:

- Discuss internally to determine your company's strengths
- Reach out to your customers and ask them questions like, "of the products and services we provide to you, which ones are we best at and why?"
- Evaluate your internal data to see what trends are emerging in terms of products and services that are growing consistently—this may give you a sense for what the marketplace values most from you

Once you determine your core competencies, look at your current customers to see who will value and benefit the most from what you do. Also, think about what other kinds of businesses might be particularly aligned with your core competencies. Consolidate all this thinking and feedback to determine your target market—those that benefit the most from the main things you do offer?

I often advise clients that if you intend to be all things to all people in the marketplace, you are setting yourself up to be nothing to nobody. In an increasingly competitive environment, specialists who are known for being very good at a limited set of skills will survive and excel.

WHAT DOES MY TARGET MARKET VALUE?

Once you determine your target market, you have to figure out what they value the most. These are called "value drivers" as they drive value for your target market. This goes way deeper than price and customer service. Examples of value drivers include but certainly are not limited to:

- Immediate response to problems
- Breadth of services
- No questions asked return policy
- Ongoing advice and consulting

Your target market has specific value drivers and it is crucial you know what they are. So, how do you find out? You employ similar methods as you did to determine your target market (above), but most importantly, you go to your existing and potential customers and ask them directly. There are three popular ways to solicit value driver information from your target market. These include:

- Set up one-on-one meetings—Meet with your existing customers and ask them, "in terms of the products and services we provide to you, what things are most important to you in our ongoing relationship?"
- Conduct focus groups—Select 10-20 people who represent your target market, get them in a group, and ask them a series of questions about what they value from a provider like you.
- Survey the marketplace—develop a survey customized to your target market and work with a third-party survey company to obtain the appropriate information.

I can't stress enough how critical it is that you really understand what your marketplace values concerning the products and services you sell.

WHAT ARE YOUR CUSTOMERS' "EMOTIONOMICS"?
You may have heard about the "experience economy". The experience economy is defined as customers paying for two things when they do business with you; 1) a great product or service, and 2) a very satisfying emotional experience while consuming the product or service.

In the experience economy "emotionomics" drive economics. Your customers pay for the products and services you sell and in return, you give them "emotional currency". If the emotional currency they get is more than the monetary currency they pay, the "emotionomics" factor is in your customer's favor – that is a good thing. This produces very satisfied customers who may promote you to others. If the "emotionomics" factor is not in their favor, you run the risk of generating an unsatisfied customer. Too many times we simply think our customers are buying our products and services when they are really buying the emotions that surround them.

WHERE DO YOUR CUSTOMERS' EMOTIONOMICS FALL—IN THEIR FAVOR OR YOURS?

The best way to figure this out is to take your customers' value drivers (described above) and simply ask them how you are performing relative to them. This is done most frequently by way of customer surveys—in person or online. Regardless, if you want to excel in an increasingly competitive environment, you must execute a consistent program that determines how you are performing on the emotionomics scale.

In most cases, your marketplace is competitive and likely becoming more so. By understanding your target market (those who benefit the most from what you do) and knowing their value drivers (the things they value most from what you do) while also ensuring emotionomics are in their favor, you set yourself up to effectively compete, no matter how tough the competition.

CREATING A UNIQUE SELLING PROPOSITION (USP)

Competition is intense in virtually every marketplace. The Great Recession of 2008 has further heightened this situation. Matthew Dixon and Brent Adamson in their book, *The Challenger Sale,* found that the scarcity of business in the months and years following "Lehman Weekend" in September of 2008 forced salespeople worldwide to up their game. Dixon and Adamson stated that salespeople who focused on simply building relationships with their buyers were losing business to salespeople who were more innovative and actually challenged the current methods of doing things—hence the "challenger salesperson".

Furthermore, Dixon's and Adamson's studies found those salespeople who focused primarily on relationship-building were the least likely to be in the elite salesperson group—the top 20%. Those that brought unique perspectives acted as an industry consultant, and challenged the status-quo were most likely to be included in the elite category.

Another principle that rose out from *The Challenger Sale* study was the concept of "creating constructive tension" with your buyer. On the surface, creating tension with your buyer may not sound like the smartest idea. However, the research we did for this book reinforced the power of challenging your buyer to think "outside the box", so to speak.

In our research, we asked the question *"if a salesperson challenges your assumptions about a business topic, how would you react?"*

- 86% of respondents would view this favorably and would be willing to listen to a different perspective

YOUR USP & COMPETITIVE ADVANTAGES—WHAT MAKES YOU SO SPECIAL?

You will read elsewhere in this book about a few ways to separate yourself from the competition - modify your communications style to match your buyer, ask good questions and listen, focus on your buyer's situation instead of your goals, products, or services. These are critical skills to master. Clearly there's more to it than that, so here I will talk all about competitive differences.

When you have a solid competitive advantage or USP and can effectively communicate it, you have a real asset that belongs on every online property, in every piece of printed material, and in every message you communicate to your marketplace. USP's separate you from the competition and give your prospects a real reason to buy from you.

Your USP is a selling message or slogan that you use to ensure customers understand quickly and easily the benefits you offer that your competitors don't. It should be succinct, direct, and if you can make it "catchy" it's all the better. Unless your clients hear your USP, they may never know why they should buy from you.

4 STEPS TO IDENTIFYING YOUR USP

Step 1—Identify your competitors, what they are known for, what they do well, and what they don't do so well. You can identify these things by observing them, researching them, and asking your contacts what they know about them.

Step 2—Figure out what your business does better than anyone else. Think about this using three criteria 1) Process, 2) Expertise, and 3) Unique Product/Service.

1. Process—Do you have a process that delivers better results and greater satisfaction than your competitors?
2. Expertise—Do you have a level of expertise that is superior to your competition and can result in better performance?
3. Unique Product/Service—Is your product or service particularly unique to a certain target customer or industry and does it produce better results?

Step 3—Determine how your advantage benefits your target customers. Customers only buy to avoid pain and to achieve some benefit. They buy what the product or service can do for them, not the features of the product or service itself.

Step 4—Write a short paragraph describing what you have revealed in steps 1-3. Read through the paragraph and condense it to a couple of short sentences that can be easily remembered and communicated verbally. An example – *"We are the only Google Certified AdWords and Analytics Partner Company in Virginia. This unique expertise produces better and more sustainable online marketing results for our customers."* This is a competitive difference for the digital marketing company I founded).

COMMUNICATING YOUR USP – SELLING DIRECT TO CONSUMERS

The best ways to communicate your USP are dependent on how your customers research, evaluate, and buy the products or services you sell. If you market and sell direct to the public (Business-to-Consumer), you like use some type of mass marketing to communicate your message. This might include radio, TV, print or online marketing. Your USP should be near the beginning and the end of your verbal messages. If you are doing TV, it should be reinforced in print on the screen and be prominent in all printed materials. On your website, your USP should be prominent without being obnoxious.

COMMUNICATING YOUR USP – SELLING TO OTHER BUSINESSES

If you are selling to other businesses, it is likely that you are involved in direct marketing or networking with your target market. This environment normally involves more direct verbal communications—cold calls, networking conversations, initial interactions with customers, etc. In this environment, your USP is critical to gain the attention of the person to whom you are speaking. Example statements sound like…

- At a networking event when asked what you do you say, *"I'm with WebStrategies. We're an online marketing company and the only Google Certified AdWords and Analytics Partner Company in Virginia. Our customers find our expertise produces better, more sustainable online marketing results."*
- During a cold call or direct marketing conversation you might say—*"I'm with WebStrategies. We provide online marketing services to firms like yours and are the only Google Certified*

AdWords and Analytics Partner Company in Virginia. Our expertise produces better, more sustainable online marketing results for our customers."

Your USP is a powerful marketing asset that will capture the attention of your target market. Follow the steps to identify what you do better than anyone else and craft a statement that is succinct, direct, and rolls off your tongue naturally.

KNOW YOUR COMPETITION

If you don't know your competitors and have a good understanding of what they are and are not good at, then how can you separate yourself from them? It's simple: You can't. It is imperative that you know your competitor's strengths and weaknesses. With this awareness, you can clearly communicate your competitive differences and will be able to make statements that *imply* your competitors' weaknesses.

Again, never disparage your competition. When you make objective and positive statements about your competition, your buyer gains confidence in you because of two things: 1) you know your competition and your industry, and 2) you are so confident about your company that you are not afraid to say something positive about the competition.

Of course, be careful not to sell your competition. Instead, make comments that *imply* their shortcomings. For example, you might say something like...

> *"We are the only company that has achieved XYZ certification demonstrating our knowledge of inventory management."* (This implies the competition has less knowledge and experience in inventory management.)
>
> *"Unlike others, we've been serving the market for more than 10 years."* (This implies the competition has less experience.)
>
> *"There is a lot of turnover in this industry and we are proud of the fact that our people have been with us for more than 5 years."* (This implies the competition's work environment is not stable)

Here are some ways to learn about your competitors:

- If you are uncertain of who your competitors are, do online research in Google and LinkedIn and go to local events or trade shows searching for similar firms.
- Visit their websites to learn about them.
- Ask your contacts what they know and who you might be able to talk to about them.

- Hire an independent firm to conduct a research study about your marketplace.
- Find former employees of your competition and talk with them.

In addition to knowing and understanding your competition, it is equally important to be aware of trends and innovations within your industry that will be of interest to your buyer. This enables you to offer unique perspectives and to separate yourself from the competition. Great sources for this are your buyer's industry publications and trade organization websites.

KNOW YOUR SHORTCOMINGS

Let's admit it—no one is all things to all people. No one can be a "10" at everything they do. We all have shortcomings and we all have areas that we need to develop and improve upon. Through the years, I have come to realize that one of the greatest strengths of any human being is awareness: being aware of the things you are and are not good at. With this knowledge, you can create partnerships with others that excel in areas where you are weaker. Trying to succeed at something that you are not good at will likely end in disappointment and poor results—things that don't exactly enhance your reputation. Being able to respond to your shortcomings is important. Before going to market, think about where you fall short, and prepare to minimize those shortcomings. Be ready to tackle a related objection if one should arise.

HOW TO BE A CONTENDER - B2B SALES—GETTING PAST 1ST BASE

Is your industry extremely competitive? Most people responding to that question will answer affirmatively. Moreover, due to the relatively low cost of entry in the B2B services sector, competition seems to constantly intensify.

How can you stand out from the competition and make it clear to your marketplace that you have the "chops" to get past first base? How will you go about getting the attention of your target market and have them view you as a firm that should be seriously considered?

Here, you will find information about how to present your company to qualified prospects and how to clearly communicate that you are a serious contender.

As part of my research for this book, buyers were asked how long a salesperson should take to present information about his or her company. Below is an excerpt from the survey:

When a salesperson is presenting information about his/her company, how long should that presentation take? (Select the item closest to your answer.)

Answer	0%	100%	Number of Response(s)	Response Ratio
5 minutes or less			50	46.7 %
5 - 15 minutes			40	37.3 %
15 - 30 minutes			15	14.0 %
More than 30 minutes			1	<1 %
No Response(s)			1	<1 %
		Totals	107	100%

While this surprises most people, it didn't surprise me at all. After many years on the buying side of sales meetings, I quickly became bored listening to salespeople showing me long slide decks and talking incessantly about their company. Buyers want to know about your firm but are far more interested in sharing their goals and learning how you can help them to achieve them.

Before we dig into the four main things buyers consider when deciding if your company qualifies for consideration, we must acknowledge and remember that the buyer has to make three important decisions before you can make a sale. These decisions are to 1) buy you as a salesperson, 2) buy your company, and 3) only after making those previous two buying decisions, to buy your products or services.

So, what are the top four things buyers consider when deciding if a B2B firm can be a contender and how can you present these in a sales meeting?

When you take just a few minutes (as few as possible) in a sales meeting to tell your buyer about your firm, here are some guidelines on how to communicate the four most important items:

- Capabilities—Does your firm have the capabilities to achieve what needs to be accomplished? When telling the buyer about your firm, simply list the main products and services your firm provides. If you've been successful at first selling yourself and the buyer seeks deeper information about what you do, he will ask.

- People—Does your firm have the depth of personnel required to achieve what needs to be accomplished? In this case, it may be helpful to show pictures of your staff and describe their capabilities and qualifications without going in depth about any one person's background. Once again, being brief shows that you value the buyer's time. Again, if the buyer has a question, he will ask.

- References—Can you cite examples of how your firm has worked on and accomplished similar challenges? Case studies and associated summaries are great ways to quickly communicate you have experience working with similar situations. To be brief, you can simply show headlines of some of your case studies and provide the whole picture if and when the buyer requests it.

- Customers—Who else have you worked with? Showing some of your other clients is a great way to communicate your experience and credibility. An easy way to do this is to make a slide or handout that shows the logos of some of your customers—as long as doing so doesn't violate your customers' privacy.

Sell yourself first and then demonstrate that your company is a solid contender. Be brief when presenting your company and focus your presentation time on the four main things that your buyer is searching for — capabilities, people, references and customers. Do these things well and you will effectively sell yourself and your company. The challenge then becomes selling your products and services.

SELL SOLUTIONS NOT PRODUCTS & SERVICES

As stated elsewhere in this book, two of the characteristics that buyers value most are *good problem solving* skills and a *demonstrated ability to solve a problem.* Buyers are looking for the leading edge and innovative and effective ways to impact their businesses. This is what they want and why they will inevitably buy. Remember, buyers purchase for two reasons and two reasons only—gain or pain.

You must ask good questions to determine the "gain" opportunities and also to uncover the "pain" points. Pain is certainly the more compelling of the two. Think about it—would you rather experience great pleasure or avoid great pain? Most people would choose the latter. Uncovering pain requires direct discussion with your buyer. Here are some questions that might help uncover pain points:

1. What is the competitive nature of your industry?
2. To what extent are you experiencing increased competition?
3. What are your competitors doing that concerns you?
4. What elements of your business are most troubling?
5. What worries you the most about growing your business?

These are all good open-ended questions that should get your buyer talking and allow you to learn how your products and services can solve their problem.

In our survey, our buyers listed *'talks too much'* and *'doesn't focus on me and my problem'* as the biggest frustrations regarding salespeople. Elite salespeople have the ability to understand the features and benefits of their products or services and they know how to translate those in a way that solves buyers' problems.

What problems do your products and services solve? How do your products and services translate into gain opportunities for your buyers? In order to effectively translate the features, functions, and benefits, you need to think about and prepare to articulate what problems you can solve and how they will make life better for your buyer. Write down and practice discussing the answers to these two important questions.

In some cases, your product or service may not be the best way to solve the problem and you are obligated (as an elite salesperson) to admit that and advise your buyer accordingly. That is how you become a trusted advisor and ultimately acquire a new customer in the future.

UNDERSTANDING YOUR BUYER'S PURCHASING JOURNEY - 4 IMPORTANT STEPS FOR MOVING PROSPECTS TO SALES

Various studies report that only about 4-7% of B2B buyers are in the buying mode for a particular product or service at any given time. Other studies report that anywhere from 55-70% of a B2B buyer's purchasing journey is done anonymously— in which the sellers are not aware. While these stats vary based on a variety of reasons, they are indicative of the typical B2B purchase journey. If B2B buyers are not always in the buying mode and much of their journey is done without the seller even knowing, how can B2B sales professionals operate to seize sales opportunities?

There are four important steps that position a B2B sales professional to capitalize on sales opportunities. These include 1) understanding your target customer, 2) providing opportunities for your target customers to interact with you, 3) nurturing relationships with your target customers, and 4) readiness to engage when the right time presents itself.

STEP 1—UNDERSTAND YOUR TARGET CUSTOMER

Your target customer behaves in certain predictable ways depending on what you sell. We refer to this as the "path to purchase" or also referred to as the "buying funnel". The image below provides a way to think about various buyers based on two criteria;

- Degree of required purchasing expertise and
- Degree of importance to the buyer's life.

Most B2B buying decisions fall into the "Considered" section. These buyers usually don't know much about the details of the product or service and their buying decision has potential risks. These kinds of purchases are infrequent and there is a great deal of anonymous research. Sellers should provide helpful information that is easily accessible and then nurture buyers throughout their purchasing journey.

STEP 2—PROVIDE OPPORTUNITIES TO INTERACT WITH YOU

As mentioned earlier, a large portion of the B2B buying process is done anonymously—online research and inquiring within the buyer's personal network of contacts. Whether the buyer begins the purchasing journey online or inquires within his network, it is likely they will ultimately go online to gather information. Understanding your target buyer, what is important to him and what problems he is trying to solve are critical pieces of knowledge you must have in order to stand out when anonymous research is complete.

Once the buyer makes his way to your website, are you offering information that helps him through his purchasing journey? Are you offering opportunities for him to interact with you? Your website should contain multiple ways for your buyer to interact. These could be videos, articles, whitepapers and case studies that provide helpful information. It could also include offering pricing information, ability to get an online quote, request for a free analysis, or the ability to request contact.

These are all opportunities to obtain contact information about the potential buyer. It is doubtful though that anyone will give you their contact information online unless you are giving information that is of great value. This is where most companies fail—the information they are offering just isn't compelling enough for people to identify themselves through the typical anonymous purchasing journey.

STEP 3—NURTURE YOUR LEADS THROUGH THE PURCHASING JOURNEY

Once you've identified a lead that appears to be qualified, "walk with them" through the purchasing journey—lead nurturing. Additionally, you may have captured qualified buyers from trade shows and networking events, or used other marketing tactics. Include them in your lead nurturing activities as well.

The key is to remember that a small percentage of your potential buyers are in the buying mode at any given time while others are active in their purchasing journey (doing research, evaluating suppliers, etc.). Elite salespeople are skilled at identifying qualified buyers, nurturing the lead and walking them through the purchasing journey.

To succeed in lead nurturing, arm yourself with resources that are valuable and helpful to your target buyer. Things like research reports, case studies, helpful articles, informational videos and other forms of compelling content. These are the resources required to stay in contact with your prospects and help them progress through their purchasing journey. Set up a schedule to contact them and periodically send helpful, timely information and other resources. There are a variety of CRMs and marketing automation tools out there to make this process efficient to execute.

By staying in contact with your buyers and providing them information that is meaningful and helpful, once they are to the point in the purchasing journey where they are ready to engage in conversation about the products or services you sell, you will likely be one of the suppliers to which they reach out.

STEP 4—BE ACCESSIBLE WHEN THE INQUIRY IS MADE

You've heard the saying "hurry up and wait". Well, there's truth to that in the B2B selling arena. You might be doing a great job of lead nurturing, but your buyer just isn't ready to make a decision—be patient. Buyers don't want to be sold; they want to buy so you are on their timetable. When they do finally decide it's time to make a decision, don't make them wait. Be appreciative of their interest and make yourself accessible to meet with them.

In summary, realize much of the B2B purchasing journey is done anonymous to you and that only a small portion of your potential buyers are in the buying mode at any given time. To succeed in B2B sales, you must have a good understanding of your customer, make it easy for him to interact with you during the purchasing journey, nurture your leads by providing helpful information, and be accessible when your buyer is ready to engage.

UNDERSTANDING THE B2B SELLING ENVIRONMENT - 4 WAYS TO GENERATE SALES LEADS IN A B2B ENVIRONMENT

A recent research study about the B2B selling environment found that nearly 70% of the buyer's journey is made anonymously in self-discovery mode with online content—not through direct marketing or sales interaction.

My personal experience over the last 10 years proves this to be accurate. I have tried just about everything you can think of and have found a formula that works. With 70% of a B2B buyer's sales journey occurring anonymously, how do companies selling to other companies generate leads? Here are the four proven methods...

ONLINE VISIBILITY—SEARCH ENGINES

Like all of us, businesses are using the internet more than ever to find and evaluate suppliers. This "anonymous journey" usually starts in two ways—doing an internet search and coming across interesting online content. Research studies find that B2B firms generate high ROI through search engine optimization (SEO). Not every firm seeks suppliers through an online search, but as people who grew up in the "internet age" become the decision-makers, online search behavior increases.

Your goal with SEO should be to rank for search phrases that are highly relevant and searched often. Optimum positioning in search results is on the first page and "above the fold"—visible without scrolling from the top. This position generally represents the 6th search listing or higher. Click-through rates on search engine results page (SERPs) erode significantly as you go down the page, and that is why showing above the fold is so important. You don't just want high rankings; you want visitors to your website.

ONLINE VISIBILITY—INTERESTING CONTENT

News feeds, social media sites, and other online properties are full of content that B2B decision-makers are consuming at a record pace. Are you producing good, interesting content? Are you sharing it online? It amazes me how often I get a call from someone who has seen one of my articles on LinkedIn. We take the approach of sharing our "best stuff" online, and it appears some of it is good enough to get noticed. Your content should be original and consist of things like articles, white papers, case studies and industry reports. When you do content marketing the right way, you are communicating your knowledge and experience to your target market. You are also gaining a competitive advantage and enhancing your credibility.

OFFLINE VISIBILITY

Are you hanging around the same places as your target market? If not, you are missing a key part of B2B lead generation. Associating with the right business groups, attending trade shows and networking with other well-connected people are critical tactics to generating leads in the B2B space. The key here is to stand out from the rest. I have specifically found that it's better to be highly visible in fewer offline venues than to just simply participate in far more.

BROADCASTING—SEMINARS AND SPEAKING ENGAGEMENTS

Just like you are sharing your "best stuff" when you do content marketing, you can make an even bigger and more personal impact when you do seminars and speaking engagements. Getting in front of your target market isn't easy, but it's an opportunity to showcase your knowledge and show people you are someone with whom they'd enjoy working. Every time I or one of our people have presented to an industry group, we've walked away with new business.

Cold calling used to be a way to get in front of targeted prospects; that doesn't work as well anymore. If you can give your targeted prospects an opportunity, for example, a discussion over lunch or an invitation-only seminar where they might gain something valuable, it's a sure-fire way to get in front of the right people and generate a strong connection.

CREATE RAVING FANS

We can read all the studies we want, but one immutable law of marketing is that positive "word of mouth" is the single most significant way to generate business. The key is through creating "raving fans" of your current customers. At my firm, our mission is to create raving fans and we talk about it all of the time. In fact, we don't want to take on a new client unless we are certain we can make that client a raving fan. Admittedly, we are not perfect and occasionally we make mistakes. But when we do, we work very hard to recover our client's trust—continuing them on that journey to being a raving fan.

In B2B selling when the project values are relatively high, buyers are discriminating and they are doing much of their research anonymously online. If you can be found in the search engines and offer good, original content that is visible to your target market, your buyer's anonymous journey online will lead them to you. Combine your online visibility with your offline visibility through networking, seminars, and speeches. Finally, a positive reputation and good word of mouth from your raving fans will put you well on your way to a continuous stream of qualified sales leads.

6 STEPS TO CREATING ENGAGING WEBSITE CONTENT AND TURNING YOUR WEBSITE INTO A SELLING TOOL

What makes a website an effective selling tool and why do some websites perform well with lead generation while others fail? There are many answers to these questions and this section focuses on how the content in your website makes all the difference.

First, consider a few questions in regards to your website...

- Can it be found in the search engines?
- When someone comes to it do they see an outdated website?
- Is it mobile-responsive and displays well on mobile devices?
- Does it meet the "credibility test"?
- Does the content create a desire that drives the customer to take action?

On the topic of content in your website, there are six steps to getting it right. Think about what is important to your target market and then develop content that walks through the AIDA cycle—Attention, Interest, Desire, and Action.

STEP 1—WHAT IS THE PERSONA OF YOUR TARGET MARKET?

Who is my typical buyer? What is important to him? How does he make decisions? What isn't important to him? Sometimes this takes research in the form of surveys, focus groups, advisory groups, and the like. Come up with the right answers and you have the foundation for excellent website content.

STEP 2—WHAT IS YOUR CUSTOMER'S PROBLEM?

People buy for two reasons and two reasons only—gain or pain. They either want to GAIN something to make their lives better or they want to avoid PAIN and keep something unpleasant from happening. Once you understand who your customer is and what is important to him, you can ask yourself...

- What is my customer looking to gain?
- What is my customer's problem for which he is seeking a solution?

When you identify the answers to these questions, you can use this information to ensure your website content addresses both the "gain" and "pain" points.

Now, you are ready to appeal to your buyer and move them through the AIDA cycle via website content…

STEP 3—GET THEIR **ATTENTION** WITH A GREAT HEADLINE

The headline goes at the top of the web-page. Let's say that you are looking for information about how to improve your selling success and come upon a web-page that discusses selling skills. Which of the following two headlines will get your attention and motivate you to continue reading?

- "Selling Skills"
- "Increase Your Close Ratio by 20% - Guaranteed"

Most people will choose the second one. Why? It clearly states a solution and likely addresses the reason that the customer is searching for help in the first place.

STEP 4—GIVE A LITTLE MORE TO GENERATE **INTEREST**

You've grabbed attention with a good headline and the customer is motivated to read on. Now is the time to give them more reasons to continue their search with you. This typically comes in the form of a sub-headline; one or two sentences that provide more information on how the service you are providing will address the customer's "pain" or "gain" points. This is often called "teaser text". Here's an example that builds on the previous headline – "Increase Your Close Ratio by 20% - Guaranteed"…

"Our customers have reported an increase in close ratio of at least 20% within 3 months after completing our courses. Learn more about how it works."

We've grabbed their attention with a good headline and now we've given a little more evidence ("teaser text") that will likely peak further interest. At this point, we only have 36 words between the headline and two sentences. A typical person can consume this amount of text in about 10 seconds.

STEP 5—CREATE THE **DESIRE** TO TAKE ACTION

With our strong headline and "teaser text", we have the customer wanting to learn more. Now it is time to share some details and this is where it gets tricky. Remember that you have determined what is most important to your customer and you now understand how he makes decisions. This knowledge will determine what features you communicate. Choose to highlight the features that make the biggest difference to your customer and also those that play a part in his decision making process. It is important that you don't feature the ones YOU think are important.

Back to our original example of the selling skills website: Here are a few effective ways of sharing details and features...

- Extensive time is applied to the three most difficult selling skills (closing skills, asking the right questions, and researching your buyer). Our unique skills development method creates real change in how these skills are implemented in live selling.
- Videotaped role playing is used extensively in the training classes which dramatically increases behavior changes and makes it easy to transfer classroom learning out into the real world.
- Post-classroom follow-up coaching sessions are used to evaluate real-life selling situations and reinforce the critical selling skills that ultimately result in a 20% improvement in close ratio.

Each of the statements includes a "feature" and also explains how the feature produces a "benefit". At this point, we've asked the customer to read 133 words, which a typical site visitor gets through in about 40 seconds.

STEP 6—TELL THEM HOW TO TAKE **ACTION**

You have gotten their ATTENTION with a great headline, you have generated some INTEREST with the "teaser text", and have also created DESIRE by articulating the features that produce the benefits that your customer is seeking. You now need to tell them what to do—how to take ACTION.

Don't leave it up to the customer to figure it out—tell them exactly how to take the next step. This final step is the "call-to-action" and is typically delivered on a website by some kind of graphic image—here's an example...

Get a Free Sample Sales Aptitude Assessment & see the power of assessments for yourself

Making sure that your website is an effective selling tool requires many things including having the right content that best appeals to your customers. Understanding what is and isn't important to your customer and then walking them through the ATTENTION—INTEREST—DESIRE—ACTION cycle, will make your website a lead producing asset for your business.

SHAPING EFFECTIVE MARKETING MESSAGES - 3 WAYS TO MAKE YOUR BUYER CONFIDENT IN YOU

In a sales meeting with a good prospect, what can you say that convinces the buyer that you are the one for the job? What statements can you make that build confidence in your buyer regarding you but that also put some doubt in your buyer's mind about the competition? Having strong marketing statements ready to help "seal the deal" or to overcome an objection is critical to separating yourself from the competition and allowing you to close the sale.

Here, I will focus on three different types of marketing messages that can be used in a sales meeting 1) the Killer Argument, 2) Key Discriminators, and 3) Ghosting Discriminators. These marketing messages have been developed by top marketers because they answer the logical and emotional questions of most buyers and allow you to differentiate yourself.

THE KILLER ARGUMENT

The "killer argument" concept comes from Dale Carnegie and focuses on communicating the fact that "you've done this before". For example: you are pitching an inventory system to a wholesaler and you say, "Earlier this year we installed a system with virtually the exact requirements for another wholesale company and they are very pleased with it." A statement like that reduces the risk your buyer might have about your capabilities.

However, there are the times that you have not done it before. A good salesperson might say something like, "one of our closest technology partners has those exact capabilities and combined with our support, you can have an inventory system that is more accurate". This doesn't have the same impact the earlier statement did, but it will likely instill some confidence with your buyer that keeps you in the deal.

As always, you want to be completely honest with your buyer and we know that no company can do it all. When you haven't done the exact thing your buyer seeks, you just need to be a bit creative in instilling confidence in your buyer and letting them know that you have the capabilities to do the job and to do it right.

KEY DISCRIMINATORS

The concept of "key discriminators" in the sales environment comes from the book *How to Become a Rainmaker* by Jeffrey Fox. The idea is similar to a competitive difference or unique selling proposition and answers the buyer's question, "why should I do business with you?", or I often ask "what makes you so special?"

You need to be able to articulate your "key discriminator". For example: my firm, WebStrategies Inc., is the only Google Search and Analytics Partner in the state of Virginia. That is a "key discriminator" that separates us from the competition.

You should carefully craft your "key discriminators". You may not have one that is truly unique to you but there are things about you and your firm that are competitive differentiators. One final note—whatever you do, do not claim your "key discriminator" is good customer service unless you can prove it. Everyone says their customer service is good but unless you can prove it, it will go in one ear and out the other.

GHOSTING DISCRIMINATORS

The concept of "ghosting discriminators" also comes from Fox's *How to Become a Rainmaker*. It relates to statements you can make that imply a weakness in your competition and puts doubt in your buyer's mind about the competition.

You never want to disparage your competition. It is much more effective when you say things that imply their shortcomings. For example: saying something like "we are the only firm that delivers on time consistently" implies that the competition does not. It puts doubt in the buyer's mind that if he chooses the competition there may be delivery problems. Another way to say this is "unlike our competition, we deliver on-time consistently".

Think about what your firm does better than the competition. Think about your competition's shortcomings. Unlike the "key discriminator", it doesn't have to be unique. Next, prepare some "ghosting discriminators" that are effective at putting doubt in your buyer's mind about the competition.

Having marketing messages like "killer arguments", "key discriminators" and "ghosting discriminators" ready to roll off your tongue at just the right moment is vital during a sales meeting. These messages instill confidence in your buyer's mind and place some doubt about your competition that will better position you to make the sale.

TESTIMONIALS - TELLING YOUR STORY THROUGH TESTIMONIALS THAT HAVE AN IMPACT

The ability to tell stories about past successes is one of the most powerful marketing tactics out there. Buyers want to have confidence that your solutions will work. What better way to seal their confidence than with specific stories of how your solutions have succeeded elsewhere? Written testimonials, video testimonials, and case studies are ways to gain the buyer's confidence.

Customer testimonials can be a powerful confidence builder but buyers will have varying views about their credibility. One of our survey questions is directly related to how customer's viewed these testimonials. When asked *"what is your view of customer testimonials – positive or negative?"* this is what we found...

1. 80% of respondents said written testimonials with the person's full name and company had a positive impact
2. 75% felt video testimonials also had a positive impact
3. 58% said written testimonials with the person's first name and industry are as good as those that included full name and company
4. Only 10% positively viewed written testimonials that did not include a name, a company, or an industry

Additionally, only 20% of respondents indicated that testimonials had no meaningful impact on them – further proof of the power of credible testimonials.

TELL YOUR STORY THROUGH CASE STUDIES

From the experience of owning a company and selling in a B2B environment for 10+years, I cannot overstate the power of case studies, especially when they are done right. As soon as you can begin creating case studies of successful results and meaningful relationships, do it. The two most powerful uses of case studies are:

- Peek the interest of prospects and set yourself apart from most of your competition
- Build confidence in the buyer about your product and services

Case studies should include:

- A good headline that captures the interest of the reader
- Description of the situation your customer was experiencing
- Clear explanation of the solutions that you offered and how they were applied
- A summary of the results achieved
- A customer testimonial

Since business success is often measured by the numbers, be as quantitative as possible when describing the results you achieve.

TOP 3 REASONS WHY YOU SHOULD BLOG

Blogging is "the bomb" and this post gives three compelling reasons why you should blog along with some suggestions on how to get started. However, first, let's get one thing straight: The phrase "the bomb" was popularized in the 90's and according to the Urban Dictionary means "exceptionally cool". Now that we've established "coolness", let's talk about why blogging is "the bomb".

A very credible player in the online space recently reported the following stats...

- 48% more traffic is generated by websites with more than 50 web-pages vs. those with fewer pages
- 67% more leads are generated by B2B marketers that blog consistently vs. those that don't
- Websites that have good blogging activity have more than four times the number of web-pages and nearly double the number of back-links vs. those websites that lack good blogging activity (you will learn later why more web-pages and back-links are good)
- Marketers who invest in blogging are 13 times more likely to achieve a positive ROI from their marketing expenditures.

Here's the deal...in most blogging platforms, each blog becomes a unique web-page. On the WebStrategies website, we have about 50 marketing and informational pages that describe a variety of ways we benefit our customers. When you ask Google how many web-pages they see when they index our website, the number is 869. How do we know this? Go to a Google search box and type in "site:(your domain name). For example, if your domain name is website.com, then you would type into a Google search box "site:website.com", and Google would show you how many "results" (unique web-pages) they see.

WHY ARE MORE WEB-PAGES IMPORTANT? THERE ARE THREE MAIN REASONS...

1. As mentioned earlier, more web-pages typically mean better information about what you do. Google loves good content because it is informative and educational to the online world—something that is very important to Google. If your site has a lot of good content specifically on a unique set of topics, Google will want to get you a lot of exposure and that means ranking your site higher in the search engine results.

2. People share good content with their friends and online communities in which they participate. When someone shares your high-quality content (blog post), they are creating a link back to your website where the content can be read. The back-linking that results from sharing your content online is like a "vote" of popularity for your website. Google likes sites that are "popular" and will often reward your website with greater visibility and higher rankings.

3. A good quantity of high-quality blog content helps to educate your target market and this gives you a competitive advantage. Think of it this way...someone is online researching services that your company provides. They come to your site and see informative blogs that can answer some of their initial questions. They then go to one of your competitors' sites and see little to no blog content. If you were that person, in your opinion, which of the two companies is better and appears more credible? Clearly, the one that helped educate you through their blog content. It seems like common-sense, right?

HOW DO YOU GET STARTED AND WHAT DO YOU BLOG ABOUT? HERE ARE SOME SUGGESTIONS...

1. First, get a blog integrated into your website. We use Wordpress because it is very easy to learn and use

2. Think about your target market's "value-drivers"—what is most important to them when evaluating products and services in your industry

3. Make a list of themes associated with #2 above

4. Do some key-phrase research to determine the best key-phrases associated with the themes you've listed

5. Pair up your key-phrases with your themes, and now you have a list of topics about which to blog

6. Make a commitment about how often you will blog and stick to it—it is hard at times, but if you blog at least once a week, you will be well ahead of the majority of websites

Once you begin blogging and feel good about the quality of the content you are creating, push it out via social networks and email marketing. Share your blogs through Facebook, LinkedIn, Twitter and other online networks relevant to your industry. Include links to your blogs in your email marketing activity. Finally, use blogs to help nurture leads through the buying process. There are so many ways to use good, high quality content.

In summary, developing blog content is hard and it is time-consuming but the value you get is tremendous. Google will likely reward you with higher rankings and your customers may find your blog content as a competitive advantage in your industry. Your blog content can also be used in your outbound marketing activity. Now, go start blogging!

TOP 5 WAYS TO USE LINKEDIN TO INCREASE SALES

Social media is a sales game-changer. In B2B selling, LinkedIn (LI) has emerged as a must-have. Several books have been written about using LI in your sales efforts and it wouldn't be difficult to write another one here. Instead, this section focuses specifically on LI and five things you can use that will improve your sales.

WHAT MAKES YOU SO SPECIAL? — YOUR LINKEDIN PROFILE

Jack Welch, former CEO of GE is quoted, "if you don't have a competitive advantage, don't compete." This principle applies to your LI profile. Following are four critical elements to your LI profile...

1. Is your profile 100% complete? If not, you lose credibility.
2. Does your profile contain popular search phrases that someone might use to search for people like you? If not, identify good search phrases and place them into your profile. Remember to always write your profile for the reader, not the search engine.
3. Do you have recommendations? If not, get them. The last time I checked, you needed at least two recommendations to have a 100% profile.
4. Does your profile stand out and present you as more qualified than the next person? If not, acquire some certifications and author content that enhances your expertise and your competitive advantages.

DO YOU PLAY WELL WITH OTHERS?—LINKEDIN GROUPS

There are more than a million different LI Groups. If you live in Turkey and graduated from VA Tech, there's a LI group for you! Why join any LI Groups? Here's why...

*   When you are a member of a group you can email anyone else in that group.
*   Participating in a group in which people in your target market participate facilitates the ability to connect with the right people

and can give you a common bond with people to whom you can add value.

- Contributing positively to a group will enhance your personal brand and increase awareness in your marketplace.
- If you are developing strong, original content that showcases your expertise, you can post that content in your various LI groups.

IT'S NOT WHAT YOU KNOW BUT WHO YOU KNOW—CONNECTING WITH PEOPLE

When you are a "1st Degree Contact" (one of your Connections) in LI, you can interact directly with that person. If you do not have an upgraded LI account, you cannot communicate directly with anyone who isn't a "connection."

When you are seeking to contact someone who isn't "connected" directly with you, find one of your "1st Degree Contacts" who is connected to the person you are seeking. Here's how to do it...

1. Type in the person's name in the search bar
2. When his/her profile appears, look to the right of the page to see how you might be connected—through someone else
3. Reach out to the person with whom you are connected and seek an introduction to the person with whom you want to contact

The image to the right is an example. I searched for Meril Gerstenmaier, who is a "2nd Degree Connection", and I see two people who are my connections (Sabet Stroman & Eric Sunberg) that are connected to Meril. So, I would reach out to Sabet or Eric and seek an introduction to Meril. It's that easy!

PEOPLE DO BUSINESS WITH PEOPLE THEY KNOW – RESEARCH YOUR PROSPECTS

When you first meet a sales prospect, it is important to build rapport. What better way to begin building rapport than to know more information about that person? Using LI and other social platforms like Facebook, Twitter, and Google +, you can find out a lot about someone.

Before you meet with that new prospect, search for them on LI. Where did he go to school? What connections do you have in common? Where has she worked in the past? This beats commenting on the fish on the wall or embarrassing yourself by making an inappropriate comment. Do your research and use it to build rapport with your buyer.

INFORMATION IS POWER – BE A LINKEDIN PREMIUM MEMBER

I suggest you pay a little extra every month to utilize LI premium services. Here are three benefits you get with an upgraded LI membership…

1. InMail (LI's email system) enables you to make direct contact with people who are not "1st connections"
2. You can see who is viewing your profile and get more information about them
3. You will have access to hundreds of additional search results and more precise search filters

Certainly there is more to using social media in your selling activities but make sure you do the basics first and utilize LinkedIn. You should look good in your profile photo, behave well when you participate in Groups, be sociable by going out of your way to expand your network using your connections, be prepared and research your prospects ahead of time, and act like an elite sales professional by using the premium LinkedIn features. Do these things along with other sales best practices, and your sales will grow.

Three

Basic Sales

If you are an elite salesperson, top 20% in your field, opportunities for you to grow your career and increase your compensation are virtually limitless.

10 SALES STATS YOU SHOULD KNOW ABOUT

The following are ten fun and interesting facts about sales and selling performance. Included are some thoughts on how to improve in these areas. If you feel a little twinge when you read some of them, it's likely because they might be a development opportunity for you.

1. Natural sales aptitude - About 50% of the results of a salesperson are due to their natural talent/aptitude. Take the time to get to know and even test salespeople before you hire them. More on compatibility and aptitude testing later.

2. Lead nurturing—66% of buyers reported that consistent and relevant communications from the company was a key influence to buy from that company. Set up and execute a solid lead nurturing work-flow to move your buyers through their natural sales funnel.

3. Phone calls—During a phone call, 82% remember you by the tone of your voice vs. what you actually said. Make sure you sound right—not just say the right things.

4. Power of inside coaches—Salespeople have an 82% success rate at seeing a new prospect when an inside recommendation is made vs. 20% from a very effective cold call. Seek out and find an inside coach who will help you close the deal.

5. Mirror and match—Only 18% of buyers will buy from a salesperson who doesn't match the buyer's personality type vs. 82% success when personality types are aligned. Identify your buyer's style and modify your approach to align to that style.

6. First impressions—When making a first impression, 55% is how you look, 38% is how you sound, and only 7% is what you say. The processing speed of your eyes is about 25 times faster than your ears. You have about 13 seconds to make a 1st impression. Furthermore, people make significant judgments about you in the first 30 seconds of meeting you. Prepare for that first meeting to make a lasting positive impression.

7. Ask questions and listen—95% of buyers state that the typical salesperson talks too much and 74% of buyers said they were

much more likely to buy if that salesperson would simply listen to them. Ask great open-ended questions and actively listen to your buyer.

8. Handling objections—When your buyer has a few objections and you can satisfy them, your success rate is 64%. The upcoming chapter on objections provides tips for successfully handling these potential challenges.

9. Buyer values—Factors of importance to buyer decisions; salesperson competence—39%, solution recommended—22%, quality of offering—21%, price—18%. Focus on ROI and how well your products and services bring value to your buyers.

10. Ask for the sale—48% of sales calls end without an attempt to close the sale and the national sales closing rate is 27%. The upcoming chapter on closing gives more insight on when to ask for the sale.

3 THINGS BUYERS LIKE, DISLIKE, AND VALUE FROM SALESPEOPLE

Following are 3 graphs that illustrate what buyers like and don't like about dealing with salespeople:

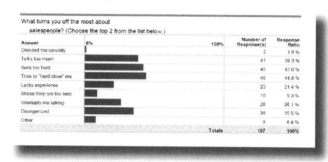

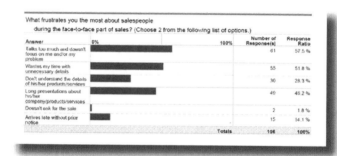

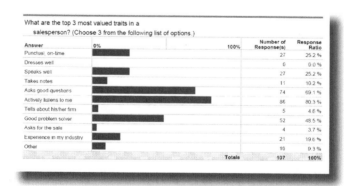

5 SALES TACTICS TO AVOID

You could read pages upon pages about what elite salespeople do but few about what they don't do. So, here's a list of five things that elite salespeople do not do.

1. IF YOU BUILD IT THEY WILL COME – NOT!

For most of us, there are meaningful competitors for the things we sell. Even if your company is a market leader, you cannot sit back and expect buyers to come to you. This may happen to some degree as a result of branding or awareness efforts, but a passive sales approach won't get you to your quota.

Prospecting is a fundamental activity for elite salespeople. Prospecting takes the form of cold calling, assertive and consistent lead nurturing activities, asking current clients for referrals, and using tools like LinkedIn to find and connect with buyers in your target market.

If prospecting is not a part of your sales and marketing efforts, it is likely you won't rank among the elite salespeople in your industry.

2. TALK ABOUT THE "FISH ON THE WALL"

Most salespeople will walk into a buyer's office, notice an interesting picture, a college emblem, or maybe even the proverbial "fish on the wall" and attempt to build rapport by talking about it. This is such a typical behavior of most salespeople that buyers can see right through it and will label you "just another salesperson".

Misinterpret one of these observations and you might be putting your foot in your mouth. I once heard about a salesperson who was attempting to build rapport with a buyer and made a comment about a picture he saw in the lobby. He said to the buyer, "I noticed that picture in the lobby of you and John Madden. When was that taken?" The buyer responded, "That is not John Madden, that is my mother." That salesperson didn't make the sale. By the way, John Madden is a former NFL football coach and announcer.

The key to sales success, like in most other business situations, is to stand out from the group and have a competitive advantage. The best way to build rapport is to research your buyer, find something business related that is unique to him, and ask a good open-ended question about that issue. This approach demonstrates you've done your homework and it will get the buyer talking.

3. SHOW UP AND THROW UP

The single biggest frustration buyers have about salespeople is they talk too much. If a buyer has invited you into his office, he wants to find out if you can actually help him or solve his problems.

The only way you can determine if your products or services can add value is if the buyer has the opportunity to explain his challenges and problems. You won't get that information by talking about yourself, your company, or your products. You learn only by asking good open-ended questions and actively listening.

During a typical sales meeting, the salesperson should be talking 30% or less. Remember the lines *a fool speaks – a wise man listens* and *God gave us two ears and one mouth –use them proportionately.*

4. BLAH, BLAH, BLAH ABOUT YOUR COMPANY

When making presentations about your company, be "short and sweet". Realize that buyers will quickly form strong impressions about you based on your appearance, tone of voice, and other non-verbal communications. Remember, simply being invited into a buyer's office is an indication you have established at least some credibility.

There's something I call the "credibility hurdle". This is the point at which the buyer determines you are credible enough to interact with. Once you've reached the "credibility hurdle", you can turn your attention to learning about the buyer's situation in order to uncover how you can add value. In other words, once you've hit the "credibility hurdle", stop trying to impress the buyer. Focus on him, not you and your company.

When it comes to telling the buyer about your company, don't go on and on. Be succinct and to the point. Spend no more than 5 minutes explaining who you are, what you do, discussing your competitive advantages, and offering information pertaining to some of the unique elements of your products and services.

5. FAILS TO FOLLOW UP

Jim Valvano, former NCAA basketball championship coach has many famous quotes about follow-up and persistence — "don't give up, don't ever give up" and "failure and rejection are only the first step to succeeding."

One of the biggest failures of most salespeople is they fail to follow-up. Buyers even express frustration about salespeople not following up after a proposal is made. It takes an average of 12 contacts to make the sale to a qualified B2B prospect. The average salesperson makes only three.

Elite salespeople follow-up until they get a "no" response. They act as though the buyer is truly interested unless the buyer specifically says "no". Elite salespeople know how to follow up without appearing to be a pest.

The best ways to follow up on a sales situation are; 1) re-emphasize the value you can add to the buyer's situation, 2) share additional/new ideas and thoughts about the situation you've been discussing with your buyer, and 3) provide education in the form of articles and resources as a means to show that you are truly interested in his success.

In summary, elite salespeople are consistently prospecting for sales opportunities. They don't sit back and let the business come to them. They build rapport by researching the buyer and asking good opening questions that build the buyer's self-esteem and get them talking. Elite salespeople ask great questions and actively listen. They seize the opportunity to learn as much as possible about the buyer and his situation. They make succinct presentations about their company and they know how to follow up. They focus on the buyer and how they can add value for him.

4 BIGGEST CONTRIBUTORS TO POOR SALES PERFORMANCE

Why do so many B2B salespeople fail? A report I recently read stated that 37% of B2B salespeople turnover each year. Absolutely staggering. But why is it so difficult to find, hire and develop a successful salesperson? After extensive experience and research on this topic, I have discovered four main reasons why salespeople don't perform as expected.

1. THEY DON'T UNDERSTAND PAIN AND GAIN

Having good product knowledge is critical but it's not the end all be all. Just as important is teaching your salespeople how the product or service you sell solves a problem for your buyer. We all have problems; we all have pain points. What problem and pain point does your product or service solve?

In our sales training classes, I drive home the point that buyers buy for two reasons and two reasons only—PAIN & GAIN.

Your salespeople must clearly understand how your product or service solves "pain" and provides "gain". Without this knowledge there's just no way your salespeople will be able to properly communicate benefits to buyers. Furthermore, it's not just knowledge of pain and gain points but the confidence that your product addresses them.

If there's uncertainty about your buyer's pain points and what they value most from the products or services you sell, you should invest in some research to determine personas, value drivers, and buyer behavior throughout the buying funnel.

2. WEAK SUPERVISION

In many ways sales is a numbers game. You see enough qualified prospects, you connect with enough people, make enough proposals, and you will make sales. Naturally you have to have good sales skills, the right attitude, and a good sales process. You also need to invest time to manage "the beast" that is hopefully inside your salesperson.

The use of lead metrics is critical. After all, you cannot manage the outcomes; you can only manage the inputs. These inputs include things like:

- How many networking events were attended and how many quality people were met?
- How many cold calls were made and how many appointments scheduled?
- How many people were added to your marketing database and how often are they touched?

You get the idea. Effective ongoing supervision of salespeople must be focused on managing the inputs—the lead activities that will result in sales. Since sales require an ongoing stream of activity, a weekly review of sales inputs is very important. In some cases, when you are dealing with a new salesperson or someone not performing well, daily reviews of inputs are necessary.

Additionally, a good salesperson is usually an optimist. If your supervision is always negative vs. constructive and developmental, you will quickly turn the optimist into a naysayer; not a trait typically found in a successful salesperson.

3. SALES PROCESS

Do you have a defined lead generation and lead nurturing sales process? If you don't, your salespeople will be far less productive. Your sales process should include the following:

- Do you have a process to generate leads? You should have multiple streams of lead generating activities. These streams may include cold calling, inbound marketing with your website, email marketing, networking events, participation in trade shows, etc.
- Is there a defined way to get those leads into a CRM? You need to have a CRM; a place where you enter all your leads and contacts. You need to be able to easily work with those leads to move them through the buying funnel. Be disciplined in maintaining your CRM.
- Do you have a lead nurturing routine? This could be as simple as touching base with the leads in your CRM. Using your CRM to do

email marketing and lead nurturing is a common activity. More sophisticated activities include marketing automation in which workflows are set up to automatically nurture leads from point of contact through sale.

- Once in front of a buyer, do you have a defined way to uncover pain and gain points and align those with the products or services you sell? Is there a standard proposal process that is supported by marketing materials and sales sheets?
- Finally, do you have a good proposal follow up process? One of the biggest reasons sales are not closed is because the salesperson doesn't follow up properly.

Without a defined sales process, a talented salesperson may get frustrated and a marginal salesperson will fail.

4. ATTITUDE—IS SALES IN THEIR DNA?

The age-old question, "are salespeople made or born" will be debated forever. You can succeed in sales without being a "natural born salesperson" but it's likely you won't be a high performer unless it's in your DNA. What traits make up that "natural born salesperson" DNA? Based on experience and research, here are the traits you should seek in finding your next successful salesperson...

- Social confidence—This is a combination of self-confidence, assertiveness, and resilience.
- Goal orientation—This is a combination of energy level, sense of urgency, and maintaining focus toward achieving a goal.
- Credibility—This is a combination of honesty, trustworthiness, and commitment to follow-through on commitments.

You need to find someone who is confident, goal oriented, and credible with a high level of energy. These are the ingredients that make up a good salesperson. One way to evaluate these along with other characteristics that measure the "natural born salesperson DNA" is testing. We use the Craft Personality Questionnaire (CPQ) to evaluate the extent to which a candidate is compatible to a sales position. There are other testing instruments out there as well but we've found the CPQ to be remarkably accurate (More on compatibility and aptitude testing later).

In summary, turnover among salespeople is staggering. There are various reasons why so many salespeople fail or find their way to "sales mediocrity". Four things are necessary to have a successful sales team. They are 1) deep knowledge about how your product or service addresses the buyer's pain and gain points, 2) disciplined and detailed leadership with a focus on lead metrics, 3) a defined sales process that is easy to execute, and 4) the right people. One can't substitute for the others; you must have all four.

7 DEADLY SINS OF SALESPEOPLE

In most industries there's no lack of competition, which means professional salespeople need to up their game. How does a sales professional selling in the B2B space up their game? One of the ways is to avoid the seven deadly sins.

My firm conducted a survey of over 100 people who make buying decisions for their companies; buying things like IT services, capital equipment and a variety of professional services. During this research we discovered things salespeople do that frustrate a buyer during the sales process. These are the seven deadly sins of salespeople.

1. TALKS TOO MUCH & SELLS TOO HARD

It's widely known that poor salespeople have a habit of "showing up and throwing up". They talk too much about themselves, their companies and their products. They make statements before asking questions. They fail to embrace one of the habits of highly successful people—"seek first to understand, then to be understood".

Our research suggests that salespeople should be talking no more than about 30% of the time, using the other 70% to ask questions that help identify challenges buyers are facing and how you may be able to solve those challenges.

2. TRIES TO MANIPULATE ME INTO SAYING "YES"

Using closing techniques like the "alternative close" or the "puppy dog close" to manipulate a "yes" turns off buyers. Research proves there's an inverse relationship between the price of a solution and the closing techniques used—the higher the price, the less closing techniques will get you the sale.

More than any other issue, the use of closing techniques turns the buyer off the most. I will go into more detail on closing techniques in a later chapter.

3. DISORGANIZED AND UNPREPARED

Showing up late, failing to properly prepare, unable to find things, and uncertain about the details of the products and services being sold—who wants to buy from this person?

Salespeople must realize the buyer has to make four decisions before buying from you, and in this particular order; 1) they buy you, 2) they buy your company, 3) they buy your product or services, and 4) they buy your price. Since they have to buy you first, if you are not organized and on top of the situation, you will never sell yourself or anything else.

4. INTERRUPTS ME WHEN I'M TALKING

As a professional salesperson, you are there to learn about your buyer and his/her business, to uncover and understand the buyer's problems, and then to figure out how your products and services can add value. You are there to ask great questions and listen actively.

In many ways, buyers take a risk in giving you information about their business. Stop coming to conclusions before the buyer is finished explaining his situation. Stop interrupting the buyer while he is talking. You are there to build rapport and learn. You will fail to do both if you are not patient while your buyer is talking.

5. WASTES TIME ON UNNECESSARY DETAILS

Our research revealed that one of the most valued traits in a salesperson is the ability to solve the buyer's problems. A salesperson has to ask the right questions, listen actively, and probe for details. There is no time to waste on things that don't add value.

Some salespeople continue to work on building rapport long after the buyer is fully engaged. This is not necessary. Continuing to explain details about the products or services that are not germane to the problem being solved just wastes time, complicates the matter, and turns off the buyer.

It's unnecessary to communicate details unless they are directly related to the solution.

Understand the buyer's problems and focus your recommendations and solutions accordingly. Don't invest time telling the buyer about all the other wonderful things your products or services can do.

6. LONG PRESENTATIONS ABOUT HIS/HER COMPANY

We asked buyers how much time a salesperson should take to tell the story about his company. Nearly 80% of respondents in our research said less than 15 minutes.

Long presentations about your company will turn your buyer off faster than anything. Don't go there. In the B2B space, buyers are interested in four main things about your company; 1) do you have the capabilities to do what the buyer thinks needs to be done, 2) do you have the personnel to do it, 3) do you have references to support your ability to do it, and 4) who else have you worked with?

Whatever presentation you make about your company, it is important to keep it short and simple and answer those four questions in the most succinct way possible.

7. THEY CALL TOO OFTEN ASKING FOR A DECISION

We asked buyers "what frustrates you the most about a salesperson's behavior between the time a proposal is presented and a decision made?" 75% of respondents said the salesperson calls too often to ask for a decision. Interestingly, slightly more than half the respondents also answered: "they forget about me". A bit of a paradox, for sure. In any case, don't do either.

In summary, we are all sinners, right? But seriously, salespeople who can avoid these seven deadly sins will position themselves as trusted advisors, build stronger rapport, and sell more valuable solutions.

TOP 10 SALES SKILLS

The internet has changed the lives of professional salespeople in a big way. Recent reports suggest more than 70% of the buying journey is done anonymously online. Combine that with more competition and instant access to information—buyers are far more empowered and educated than they were only a few years ago.

All of this raises the stakes for B2B salespeople. Here's what I believe to be the top 10 skills for a successful salesperson, including some related resources.

1. QUALIFY YOUR BUYERS EARLY

The best salespeople are ardent qualifiers. They understand what makes a qualified buyer, they know what questions to ask and how to strategically ask them to get the right information, and they know how to say "no". Successful salespeople qualify early and often and they devote their energies to only qualified buyers.

In our sales training classes, I speak about the BARTS method for qualifying buyers.

B—do they have the budget?
A—do they have the authority?
R—is there good revenue potential?
T—will they make a timely buying decision?
S—does my solution truly add value?

More on the BARTS method in a later chapter.

2. RESILIENCE TO OVERCOME REJECTION

Most successful salespeople are eternal optimists that believe most situations will turn out positive. When problems or negative situations occur, you lose a sale, or someone says "no",, a top salesperson can set these rejections aside knowing they are inevitable in the world of selling.

3. RESEARCH YOUR BUYER AND THEIR COMPETITION

The internet makes this pretty easy and the impact this makes on your buyer is meaningful. In the sales process, the buyer has to buy you first. Only after buying you, will they even consider buying your company and then your product or service. Becoming a trusted advisor is the first objective you have with any buyer (see #7 below). Don't stop with just learning about the buyer and his company. Check out his competition as well and try to identify competitive differences that may be a gain or pain point for your buyer.

4. LISTENING SKILLS ARE THE MOST VALUED TRAIT

In my research, I found that buyers place listening skills at or near the top of the traits they find most valuable in a salesperson. Salespeople should be talking 30% or less of the time. The remainder should be devoted to asking great open ended questions and listening closely (more on listening in the Questions chapter).

5. ABLE TO HANDLE AND OVERCOME OBJECTIONS

Studies say that you have a better chance of closing a sale when the buyer raises an objection and you successfully handle it versus no objection being raised at all. The first step to successfully handling objections is to recognize them. By doing so, you can prepare for how to overcome them. The next step is to follow a process for acknowledging, validating, and then overcoming the objection.

6. PRESENTING INFORMATION ABOUT YOUR COMPANY AND SOLUTIONS

Short, simple, and straightforward are the characteristics successful salespeople use. Our research suggests that you shouldn't spend more than about 5-10 minutes telling a buyer about your company. The use of printed sales materials and PowerPoint presentations is good, but make them short, simple, and straightforward. Buyers want to talk about their situation and challenges. They do not want to listen to long presentations about you.

When you are developing proposals, format them as talking points. You will be much more successful in using the proposal as a means to educate the buyer about what you can do for them than you will be in presenting thousands of words that will cause your buyer's eyes to glaze over.

7. BECOME A TRUSTED ADVISOR

As a successful salesperson, the first persona you should assume is that of a trusted advisor. As stated earlier before the buyer can buy your product or service, he must first buy you. Trust between you and your buyer is achieved in the following ways:

- Have knowledge about their business and industry so they trust that you can effectively apply your products and services to their business.
- Actively listen so the buyer knows you are correctly interpreting and understanding what he is telling you.
- Convince the buyer that you won't do anything that is not in his best interest, even if that means not selling as much as possible.

8. GET REFERRALS

"Warm" referrals are great for any salesperson. The best way to get referrals from existing customers is to serve them well. After that, develop a good way to ask for referrals and be sure to practice so it comes off natural and non-threatening. Here's an example of a way to ask for a referral...

"I'm thrilled that you are pleased with how we've served you. If you know anyone else that you think we can bring value to, warm referrals are always appreciated. Can you think of anyone at this point?"

9. CASE STUDIES AND EXAMPLES

Having case studies and stories on hand is an effective way of informing your buyer about how you operate and showing them the results you are able to achieve. Most buyers don't mind talking about concepts but when you can back them up with real examples and stories, your credibility and relationship with your buyer ascends to a new level.

10. CLOSING SKILLS

Closing the sale is not an event in and of itself. Rather, it is a series of steps that lead you to the right time to ask for the sale. It starts with trial closings, a series of open-ended questions that enable you to gauge where your buyer is in the buying journey. After that, it becomes a matter of being able to identify buying signals. When you have responded appropriately to your buyer's questions and objections and you are also picking up the right buying signals, it is time to ask for the sale.

10 THINGS BUYERS WANT FROM SALESPEOPLE

Selling to other businesses has many unique elements—some of which may include: a more sophisticated buyer, a more complex situation, multiple buyers, clearer expectations of performance, and your reputation being on the line. Connecting with these buyers by way of giving them what they want is a sure fire way to get their business.

Based on personal experience, my own proprietary research, and exposure from books and sales training programs, following are the top 10 things buyers want from B2B sales consultants:

1. Be prepared—Buyers will notice how much prep work you have done to learn about their industry and their companies. While good prep work may not ultimately win you the business, it sure can set you apart from the competition. Early in my sales career, before we built compelling competitive advantages, I'd go out of my way to dazzle the buyer with my knowledge about them and their businesses. I have no doubt that my prep work won many projects.

2. Let the buyer do the talking—Let them talk about their company, their problems, their challenges, etc. Our proprietary research supports this 100%. When we asked B2B buyers what they valued most from salespeople, they said the ability to ask good questions and listen. I cannot emphasize enough that salespeople should be listening actively—talking less than 30% of the time.

3. Be a consultant from the beginning—I am a great fan of *The Challenger Sale* concepts. The research is among the most extensive relative to selling B2B. Buyers today expect you to consult with them from the very beginning. Unless you can share some wisdom about how to solve their problems, it is doubtful you will get the deal. Givers gain.

4. Educate the buyer—The buyer is going to expect you to bring something new to the table—information, wisdom, a unique perspective, etc. Buyers will also expect you to share the ways you have helped others like them solve similar challenges.

5. Be sympathetic to the buyer's challenges—Buyers have problems too and all too often they just need to vent. Listen carefully and be empathetic/sympathetic to their challenges. This will accelerate your emotional connection with the buyer.

6. Ask really good questions—As mentioned in #2 above, beyond all else, buyers value a salesperson's ability to ask profound questions and listen carefully. When a buyer once commented to me "none of your competitors asked these kinds of questions", I quickly learned that the depth and relevance of my questions could distinguish me.

7. Explore why they are doing what they are doing—Buyers want you to understand them and their businesses. A lack of understanding is one of the biggest reasons that buyers buy from someone else. There's no better way to understand their current situation and to determine how you can add value more than exploring deeply what they are currently doing and why they chose their current methods. In our research, we found that 86% of buyers would have a favorable view of the salesperson if the salesperson challenged the buyer's assumptions about his business. Of course, you had better be able to thoroughly back up your position on the matter.

8. Provides options, explains advantages and disadvantages—Our proprietary research supports this as well. When we asked buyers if they'd prefer being presented with options vs. recommendation of a single solution, 84% said they wanted to see options. Remember, buyers don't want to be sold—they want to buy. Giving options allows the buyer to decide what he wants to buy. Do this well and you may also increase your average order size.

9. No closing techniques—We would all like to close as quickly as possible but in the B2B selling space, we should be satisfied with simply moving successfully to the next step. In our research, we asked about closing techniques. Buyers responded that hard and manipulative closing techniques turned them off. Asking them "how do you want to move forward from here" or "what would

you like the next step to be" are closing methods that will keep things moving in the right direction and likely win your business.

10. Don't interrupt the buyer, but he can interrupt you—When we asked buyers to identify what turns them off about salespeople, one of the top answers was "interrupts me when I'm talking". I know I am being redundant here, but go back to points #2 and #6. No more needs to be said about asking good questions and listening well.

In summary, buyers want to be heard. They want to be understood. They have problems just like you and I and sometimes they need to vent. Be prepared. Give and educate as ways to get—givers gain. Explore by asking really good questions and provide options for solving the situation. Don't try to close before the time is right. Be satisfied by simply moving to the next phase in the buying process. Do these things and you will be rewarded with greater success.

WHAT BUYERS SAY ABOUT SALESPEOPLE

As part of writing this book, I conducted a survey of more than 100 people who make buying decisions for their businesses every day. I was curious as to what behaviors and skills are valued the most and also the least. I wanted to learn what they saw as the best way to accomplish sales goals. Lastly, I wanted to understand what turns off a buyer the most. I asked and here's what I found...

WHAT ARE THE MOST VALUED TRAITS IN A SALESPERSON?

- Actively listens to me—80%
- Asks good questions—69%
- Is a good problem solver—49%

A salesperson learns nothing about the buyer's goals, challenges, and problems by talking and going through sales literature or making PowerPoint presentations. The salesperson needs to start off by building rapport and then ask good open ended questions. Still, listening remains, by far, the most important.

WHAT IS THE BEST WAY TO BUILD RAPPORT AND TRUST WITH A BUYER?

- Demonstrate competence by asking good, open ended questions—87%
- Open with small talk about current events—23%
- Open with small talk about things personal to me—21%

Do you see a pattern starting here? The best way to build rapport and trust is to ask good questions and listen. Sometimes, the buyer is a little resistant because they may feel guarded or uncomfortable sharing everything with you. Brief small talk at the beginning of a sales call is important. Once there is open communication, start asking questions and listening. Buyers have objectives and problems just like salespeople do and the only way to help them achieve those objectives is to hear the buyer explain them.

HOW MUCH TIME SHOULD I TAKE TO TELL THE BUYER ABOUT MY COMPANY?

- 5 minutes are less—47%
- 5-15 minutes—37%
- 15-30 minutes—14%

Nearly half the buyers that we surveyed suggested you take no more than five minutes to tell them about your company. What does that tell you? It tells me that it's not about me and my company – it's about the buyer and what he's trying to achieve. Don't waste time on lengthy presentations about your company. Instead, share some details and competitive advantages to set the stage and begin learning about your prospect.

WHAT SKILLS ARE MOST EFFECTIVE AT SEPARATING A SALESPERSON FROM HIS/HER PEERS?

- Demonstrates ability to solve my problem—64%
- Asks good questions and listens well—48%
- Understands my business—42%

This is consistent with being the most valued traits of a salesperson. The ability to not only ask good questions but also the right questions, that will help you to understand the problem and the business, is critical to becoming an elite salesperson.

WHAT FRUSTRATES YOU THE MOST ABOUT SALESPEOPLE DURING FACE-TO-FACE INTERACTIONS?

- Talks too much and doesn't focus on my problem—58%
- Wastes my time with unnecessary details—52%
- Long presentations about his/her company—46%

Now I know it sounds like I am beating a dead horse here. Clearly, buyers have a need to express themselves and they want to explain their problems and challenges. They don't want to waste their time listening to long presentations about your company. They want you to ask questions that no one else has asked them so that you can prove that you understand their business and the issues they face better than anyone else.

The ability to ask the right questions in the right manner and actually hear the answers is the second most difficult selling skill to master—after effective closing skills. When you do talk about your company, focus on what you do and be able to present a couple of competitive advantages. Then dive head-first into learning about your prospect.

STRATEGIES AND TACTICS TO ACQUIRE NEW CUSTOMERS

B2B buyers are tougher and more discerning than they were a few years ago. Why? Many experts say it is because of the Great Recession, which started in 2008 and still lingers to some degree today. Since that time, selling into the B2B space has become more difficult. Buyers are more demanding and less likely to open their checkbooks. Investments need to make sense and in many ways, you need to prove yourself on a small scale before acquiring larger orders.

This all makes acquiring new customers difficult. In light of a more challenging economic and selling environment, it takes some creative thinking to achieve your sales goals. Below, I discuss a proven three-step strategy w for acquiring new customers. It's about your willingness to start small knowing that you will finish big. This outlines how to make it easier for buyers to do business with you.

STEP 1—DEVELOP A HIGH VALUE, LOW INVESTMENT PRODUCT OR SERVICE

The first step in this proven strategy is to start small. Develop a lower cost, entry level product or service that aligns with your overall product offering. In some cases, you might want to provide a "free trial" if that makes sense for your business. To figure out the low cost product or service, do a little bit of research on your part:

1. Determine your buyer's value drivers—what is most important to him/her?
2. Evaluate the elements of your larger service offering and identify scaled down pieces that you can do independently.
3. Assemble some alternatives and get feedback from trusted advisors.

Throw all of this information into your "mental bucket", stir it around and come up with a product or service offering that has the following characteristics:

- It has high value and low risk for the buyer.
- The investment is relatively low compared to other services in your industry.
- It is aligned with your core offering and is a solid representation of your full offering.
- It gives the buyer an opportunity to see how well you are able to service them.

STEP 2—DEVELOP YOUR MARKETING PLAN AND MATERIALS

The next step is to develop marketing materials that describe this service in a compelling way. These materials should be a combination of offline and online assets, and may include, but not be limited to the following:

- Versatile sales sheet that you can hand out to qualified prospects in a variety of sales venues.
- Landing page in your website that describes the benefits of this service.
- A video that quickly explains what the service is and how it works.
- Brief PowerPoint presentation that you can show in sales meetings.
- Email piece that has a compelling subject line and headline, and links them to the landing page.

STEP 3—MAKE PEOPLE AWARE OF YOUR NEW PRODUCT OR SERVICE

How and when do you offer this new product or service? Following are some suggestions about how to market this new offering:

- Educate people in your network about the value it adds.
- Create an email campaign to your database making people aware of the new product or service.
- Write a blog post and share it throughout your online social channels.
- During sales meetings, if the buyer is qualified but not yet ready for your full program, present your new offering to them.

You can acquire more new customers by reducing your buyer's risk of doing business with a new supplier. Offering a low investment, low risk, high value product or service is one proven method that works. Develop your new product or service based on some research, and then pull together the right marketing assets that describe the value it brings. Lastly, spread the word about it throughout your offline and online channels. Do these things and you will increase the number of new customers that you acquire.

A 10-STEP PLAN FOR CAPTURING THE BIG SALE

Ask any B2B sales professional this question—Would you rather land one $50,000 sale or 10 $5,000 sales?" and most would choose the big one. The bigger the sales opportunity, the more prepared and dedicated you need to be. Closing a big sale requires an organized sales process. Once you identify the big opportunity and determine why your products and services are a good fit, we recommend the following 10-step approach to close the deal.

STEP 1—IDENTIFY WHAT IS UNIQUELY IMPORTANT TO EVERY SINGLE BUYER

At first glance, you may think there is only one decision-maker, but think again. In larger organizations, there are up to four buyer types in the decision process. These include:

- Economic/Strategic Buyer—Likely the one with the most authority because the results will impact him/her the most. This could be a VP of Marketing or Finance or some other organizational group.
- User Buyer—Likely someone operationally or project focused that may be the main user of the product or service. This person probably reports to the Economic/Strategic Buyer.
- Technical/Systems Buyer—This is someone who has a stake in the game because the solution affects other company systems for which he/she may be responsible for managing.
- "Coach"—The person inside the organization who is your "coach"—someone on your side who wants you to get the sale. This is a critical and often overlooked element.

In addition to accurately identifying the various buyers within the organization, you will also need to determine their individual needs and goals as well as identify what is important to them.

STEP 2—UNDERSTAND THE NEED AND HOW TO SATISFY EACH OF THE BUYERS

You understand the various "buyers" and that your products/services can add value to the organization. Now you must think about how you will customize your messages to satisfy the needs of each buyer. Clearly your "technical buyer" is going to seek things that are different from those sought by your "user buyer".

STEP 3—GET A GRASP OF THE FINANCIALS

What do you think the customer is spending currently on related products or services? Is their budget based on annual revenues and profit estimates? How much will your solution cost and what are the revenue gains and cost savings for your customer?

Calculate the estimated ROI of your solution and understand how long it will take for your customer to generate a 100% return on their investment. After all, "hard ROI" probably represents the most compelling reason your customer should buy.

Finally, understand the investments it will take on your end to win the deal. Naturally, if the time and expense required to gain the business is significant in comparison with the gross margin your company will gain, you might need to reconsider.

STEP 4—YOUR COMPETITION

With whom are you competing for the business? Who is the incumbent, if there is one? What do they do and not do well? How is your solution superior? These are important questions you must be able to answer in order to tailor your message during the sales process (see Steps 2 and 6).

STEP 5—WHAT INVESTMENTS DO YOU NEED TO MAKE?

A lot goes into winning a big contract—time, materials, research, etc. You need to determine what is needed to complete this process and who should be involved in getting each element completed. As stated earlier, if the task is too daunting or expensive, you should reconsider. Additionally, determine who will be the lead contact for each of the buyers and whether or not this is a deal that is worthy of their time investment.

STEP 6—WHAT ARE YOUR MARKETING MESSAGES?
Your marketing messages will be a "make" or "break" element. You need to craft three types of marketing messages as follows:

1. Your "killer argument"—This demonstrates you have the capability to do the job. Perhaps it's an example of how you did it for another company or maybe a case study that describes a similar situation.
2. Your competitive difference—At some point in the process you will need to articulate why your product or service is superior. Getting this message chiseled to perfection is critical.
3. Your "ghosting discriminators"—What can you say about your products or services that implies a weakness in the competition?

STEP 7—YOUR PRE-SELL CONTACT PLANS
What will be your contact plan during the pre-sale process and how will you customize it to reach each of the "buyers" (see Step 1)? Will you reach them through your "inside coach", use a "drip campaign", make direct contact, or use another way to get the communications started? Don't launch the first contact until you have thought through your entire communications plan.

STEP 8—WHAT ARE BUYERS' QUESTIONS AND OBJECTIONS?
What questions will each of your buyers have about you, your company, and about your products/services? What objections might each have before considering your company? Being prepared to address these questions and objections will enable you to communicate confidently and effectively.

STEP 9—WHAT ARE THE DETAILS OF YOUR SALES PRESENTATION?

When you have an audience to formally pitch, what are the most important elements of that presentation? You will certainly want to think back about Steps 2, 6 and 8. Addressing what is most important to each of the buyers (Step 2), sending the right marketing messages (Step 6), and proactively responding to the questions and objections you predict (Step 8), will likely result in a successful pitch...or will at least be one that makes them say "wow!".

STEP 10—WHAT ARE THE OPTIMAL CLOSING APPROACHES?

There are millions of ways to ask for the sale. Which ones are you prepared to execute? "Window of Opportunity", "Pilot Project", "Alternative Close", etc. Choose 2-3 potential closing methods and predict the reaction you might get from each buyer.

When going after the big sale, follow this 10-Step process and you will be surprised with how much your closing rate increases.

B2B SELLING PERFORMANCE – THE 5 FACTORS TO BE AN ELITE SALESPERSON

Are elite salespeople made or born? That is a question I get frequently. Without a doubt, there are natural born salespeople. There is no guarantee that a natural born salesperson will become an elite salesperson within your company. There is a lot more to it than that.

To answer the question, "are elite salespeople made or born?", my answer is "yes", and this article provides a roadmap for finding and supporting elite salespeople.

First, let's define "elite salesperson". Based on my experience and what I have learned, an elite salesperson performs in the top 20% of his/her class. In a Harvard study of salespeople, it was found that 62% of products and services sold in the B2B marketplace were sold by 20% of the salespeople. Consequently, we will define "elite" as the top 20%.

There are 5 factors to becoming an elite salesperson:

1. Solid understanding of your products/services and how they solve problems for your target customers
2. Selling and communications skills that enable the person to uncover problems along with the implications associated to those problems
3. Sales process that is defined and efficient, and the right tools to support the process
4. Motivating sales incentive plan and a culture that values growth
5. Natural aptitude to sell

PRODUCT KNOWLEDGE

There is absolutely no substitute for knowing your product and service. It goes way beyond just the features and benefits. The salesperson needs to understand the following elements:

1. What are the most frequent and relevant problems the target customer has that relates to your products and services?

2. What are the emotions your customers experience relative to the types of products and services you sell?
3. How do your products and services solve the most relevant problems for your target customers and what are the main benefits your customers will experience?
4. What are the ways that your products and services work and how will you articulate the details so that you can solve the customer's main problems?

Good customer research and personifying your customers will reveal answers to some of these questions. Other answers must come from learning the details of your products and services.

SELLING AND COMMUNICATION SKILLS

Selling skills are not much different than having good, basic communication skills. Here are the main selling skills required to be an elite salesperson:

- How to build rapport with a buyer and be seen as genuine and unique.
- How to combine open-ended and closed-ended questions to uncover problems you are able to solve.
- How to increase the value of your products and services by understanding the implications of the buyer's problems?
- How to listen effectively and communicate empathy to your buyers.
- How to ask trial closing questions to gain a deeper understanding of how well you are connecting with your buyers.
- How to ask for the sales without appearing manipulative or pushy.

These kinds of skills are best developed in dedicated training and development sessions and by observing live, mocked-up role-play scenarios.

GOOD SALES PROCESS AND THE RIGHT SALES TOOLS

A good sales process is comprised of several things. This includes marketing and branding, technology, a refined sales sequence, and various other items. Following are the most important elements to having a sales process that supports having elite salespeople:

1. Have you carefully constructed the right marketing and branding messages that will allow you to connect to the emotional elements and problems your target customers are experiencing?
2. What is your firm's reputation in the marketplace and do you have a unique selling proposition that resonates with your target customers?
3. Do you have an effective CRM and marketing automation platform, like Hubspot, that contains and utilizes information about your prospective customers?
4. Do you have an effective prospecting strategy that allows you to get in front of qualified buyers on a consistent basis?

Your sales and marketing strategy and process will evolve over time and can be developed more quickly by working with a company that has expertise in both marketing strategy and sales management.

SOLID AND MOTIVATING CULTURE AND PEOPLE

Many would argue that people must be self-motivated, and I agree. However, your policies, practices, and work environment will influence motivation. Here are some factors to consider about whether your work environment supports elite salespeople:

1. Do your people feel that they can grow and reach the pinnacle of Maslow's hierarchy of needs?
2. Are you recognizing the right behaviors...the behaviors that lead to sales success, good customer service, and employee growth and development?
3. Does your compensation plan offer effective reward systems?

4. Does your work environment enable individuals to express and apply their unique personal styles, skills, and abilities?

If you can answer "yes" to these questions, then you probably have a strong company culture. It is likely a relatively well-motivated group of individuals within an environment that attracts, retains, and develops elite salespeople.

NATURAL APTITUDE TO SELL

You may have a good sales process with the right tools. It may be a motivating work environment with a solid way to train and develop each person's selling skills and product knowledge, but, if you don't have salespeople with high sales computability factors, you likely won't have elite salespeople on your team. This is where pre-employment screening and assessments are key.

To hire salespeople who have "selling in their DNA", you should include some kind of sales assessment tool during the hiring process. I have used many in my career to assess salespeople and found the Craft Personality Questionnaire, or CPQ, to be the best indication of natural sales talent.

In summary, there are five factors to being an elite salesperson and one of them is simply a natural aptitude for sales. The remaining four consist of strong product knowledge, knowledge of selling skills, a good sales process that effectively incorporates the right sales tools, and a motivating work environment.

HOW TO INFLUENCE THE 5 FACTORS TO BE AN ELITE SALESPERSON

Elite salespeople are considered the top 20% in their respective space, and there are five factors that are paramount to becoming elite. Here's how you can influence the positive development of those five factors.

Factors of Success	How to Influence
• Product Knowledge—how well does this person understand the product?	• Education and training on the product/service features, functions, benefits and customer value
• Selling/Communication Skills—how well does this person understand how to sell and communicate value?	• Education and training on the top selling skills of the industry and an understanding of how to communicate to different personalities
• Motivation to Perform/Excel—how motivated are they to perform at the highest levels?	• Using reward, recognition and compensation systems to motivate the behaviors that result in superior performance
• Sales Process—has the sales process been organized and refined, and is it a repeatable and teachable process?	• Developing and refining a prospecting/ sales process that is repeatable and effective in communicating value and closing sales
• Aptitude—does the individual have a natural aptitude for sales?	• This factor can't be influenced because it is part of the person's own nature

Top salespeople are made by way of having thorough product knowledge, understanding the sales process, having great communication skills, being motivated to perform, and having an organized, refined selling process. Ultimately, if someone doesn't have the natural aptitude to be a top performing salesperson, training and education won't solve that shortcoming.

Tom Rath, author of the bestselling book *StrengthsFinder 2.0,* through many studies found that people are better off capitalizing on and developing the things that they are good at versus trying to overcome their deficiencies. In the end, focusing on strengths will lead to better performance and greater engagement—another reason why natural sales compatibility is crucial to becoming a top performing salesperson.

Management has the ability to influence everything except for natural aptitude. Many studies of human mental ability have found that our natural aptitudes are formed around the age of 12. Clearly, it would be quite the challenge to develop someone into an elite salesperson who doesn't have that natural sales aptitude.

"RELATIONSHIP BUILDER" ISN'T THE BEST SALES STYLE?

According to the extensive study that we conducted for this book, B2B salesperson behaviors were organized into five types and defined as follows:

- Hard Workers—Through sheer will, long hours, and dedication, this type of salesperson is able to succeed.
- Challengers—Researches the customer and its competition, and focuses on building constructive tension to push the customer out of his/her comfort zone.
- Relationship Builders—Creates a strong personal relationship with the buyer and nurtures that relationship over time to maximize sales.
- Lone Wolf—Breaks most of the rules, goes his/her own way and typically achieves success through unconventional, individualized effort.
- Reactive Problem Solver—Focuses energy on identifying the customer's current problem, then communicating how his/her product or service can solve it.

One of the most significant findings from the studies supporting *The Challenger Sale* is that the "Relationship Builder" sales style, thought to be the most effective, is actually the least likely style among elite salespeople. Dixon's and Adamson's studies of *elite performers (top 20%)* compared to *core performers (middle 60%)* resulted in the following summary:

Sales Style	% Elite – Those performing in top 20% in their respective firms	% Core – Those performing in the middle 60% in their respective firms
Hard Worker	16%	22%
Challenger	39%	23%
Relationship Builder	8%	26%

Lone Wolf	25%	15%
Reactive Problem Solver	12%	14%

Their studies revealed that only 8% of B2B salespeople practicing the "Relationship Builder" style were performing in the top 20% of their firm—the lowest among all of the sales types. On the flip side, 39% of B2B salespeople practicing the "Challenger" style were performing in the top 20%. It is very important to remember that Dixon's and Adamson's studies were in B2B environments where the sales process is relatively complex—those dealing with multiple levels of an organization where the average sale size is in the tens of thousands to multi-million dollars.

In my survey, I ask participants the question, "If a salesperson challenges your assumptions about a business topic, how would you react?" As we think about the "Challenger" type, the results are not surprising:

- 92% of respondents answered favorably indicating they are willing to listen to a different perspective

WHAT DOES A CHALLENGER DO?

Here's a brief summary of the "Challenger" style behaviors:

- Does extensive research on the customer and his/her competition
- Understands the customer's economic and value drivers
- Has a good understanding of how the customer conducts business
- Acts as a business consultant for the customer from the very beginning
- Creates constructive tension by pushing the customer out of their comfort zone
- Offers unique and innovative perspectives
- Is skilled and comfortable discussing the customer's sales, profits, economics, etc.

This all makes sense. Take the scenario of a "Relationship Builder" and one of his/her customers. A "Challenger" comes in and shares a unique perspective never before presented by a "Relationship Builder" and that perspective has a positive economic impact on the customer. That customer will no doubt pay close attention to what the "Challenger" has to say. Because of the criticality of the economics, that customer will likely do one of two things: 1) go back to the "Relationship Builder" and ask why he/she hasn't presented this type of solution, or 2) simply begin buying from the "Challenger". Neither case is positive for the "Relationship Builder's" credibility and future success.

In summary, the world of B2B selling has changed and the behaviors of the most elite salespeople have had to evolve to remain relevant, competitive, and highly successful.

SELL MORE TO EXISTING CUSTOMERS - HOW TO DEVELOP AND USE AN OPPORTUNITY CHART

Clearly, one of the most challenging elements of sales is getting in front of qualified leads. A great salesperson with terrific selling skills won't succeed without a steady diet of qualified prospects with whom to speak. One of the most often overlooked lead generation opportunities is your existing customers. Here, I will talk about how to systematically identify qualified leads from your current customer base.

It is well known that selling to an existing customer is 6 to 7 times less expensive and time consuming than acquiring new customers. They know you, trust you, and you already have a track-record of good performance. You know their business and they know yours. There will be no blind-dating here—you are in a position to get serious.

One of the best ways to identify sales opportunities with existing customers is to create an Opportunity Chart. An Opportunity Chart is a matrix of existing customers, what they have purchased from you, and what opportunities exist to sell them additional products and services. Here's an example of an Opportunity Chart in which the products/services are simply listed in order...

Sales Opportunity Chart - XYZ Company
(by Product/Service)

Customers	Customer 1	Customer 2	Customer 3	Customer 4	Customer 5	Customer 6	Customer 7	Customer 8
Products/Svcs								
Product 6								
Product 5								
Product 4								
Product 3								
Product 2								
Product 1								

Green = Already Sold, White = Opportunity for New Sale

Here's an example of an Opportunity Chart in which the products/services are listed by the amount of profit margin and the value in each product/service...

Sales Opportunity Chart - XYZ Company
(by Product/Sevice Margin)

Customers	Customer 1	Customer 2	Customer 3	Customer 4	Customer 5	Customer 6	Customer 7	Customer 8
Products/Svcs								
Top Margin								
High Margin								
Good Margin								
OK Margin								
Low Margin								
Loss Leader								

Green = Already Sold, Yellow = Not Sold, White = Opportunity for New Sale

Looking at sales opportunities to existing customers by profit margin and value will enable you to fine-tune your presentation and selling approach. In the above example, you see that Customers 5 and 8 have only purchased the "Loss Leader" product. Since each of these products build value from the previous product, you can present the higher margin, more valued products as the next logical step in the progression of the relationship with that customer.

Here's a more specific example of sales opportunity by margin/value. In our sales assessment and training business, we usually begin with sales compatibility assessments of individuals. This is a low cost, relatively low margin product—our "loss leader" so to speak—and establishes a basis for how individuals can improve their sales success. The next natural product or service in which an individual can improve is participation in our Top 10 Selling Skills seminar. This continues to generate higher gross margin dollars. Next, the individual and/or company participated in our 2-day Sales & Marketing Best Practices workshop, which generates higher gross profits. It is simply a natural progression of products and services.

In summary, before you go trekking off to find new sales prospects, look first in your own "backyard" and create an Opportunity Chart with your existing customers. It will be easier to approach them since you already have a good relationship built on trust, and you will seize opportunities to add greater value to them while generating more sales for you.

CALCULATING HOW MANY LEADS YOU NEED TO ACHIEVE YOUR GOALS

Too often, salespeople and sales organizations jump into the marketplace without a clear vision of where they need their numbers to be and how to consistently get there. They don't know their close rate; how many face-to-face meetings are necessary before making a proposal or how many qualified prospects it takes to make a sale. These are critical metrics to track and if you are not tracking them now—get started!

Here's an example of the importance of knowing your numbers. Let's say you have been tracking some of your metrics and here is what you have...

- Your close rate is 40%
- About 1 in 3 prospects you talk to is qualified (we'll talk about qualifying later)

How many prospects do you need to see every month in order to make one sale per week? The answer is about 32. Here's the math...

You will close 1 of every 2.5 qualified prospects you see and it takes 3 prospects to find a qualified one. Multiply how many qualified prospects you need to see by how many total prospects you see before having a qualified one. There are 4.3 weeks in a typical month, so you need to multiply the number of total prospects by 4.3 to determine how many prospects you need to see in a given month to make one sale per week.

- X 3 = 7.5 X 4.3 weeks = ~32

If your quota is based on revenue dollars, then determine your average revenue per sale and factor that into the equation. For example, let's say that your monthly sales quota is $100,000 and your average sale is $15,000. You will need to make about 7 sales per month to hit your quota.

Using the same math as in the previous example, you will need to see about 53 total prospects throughout the month to hit your numbers.

By knowing your numbers, you can begin to manage your prospecting activities accordingly. All of your marketing, lead generation, and prospecting activities should be focused on seeing the number of people you need to see to meet your goals.

UNCOVERING YOUR BUYER'S BUDGET

Experienced salespeople know that finding out what the buyer's budget is, is often a big challenge. I have experimented with several ways to ask the buyers about his/her budget. Experienced buyers will be elusive about this and some will even lie about their budget — "low-balling" it.

In my survey of buyers, I asked a question about discovering the buyer's budget. The question was, "How comfortable are you telling a salesperson what your budget is for a certain product or service?" Here's what they said...

- "Somewhat comfortable—the salesperson should have an idea but I don't want to reveal any specific numbers"—50% of respondents.
- "Very comfortable—he/she should know what my budget"—27% of respondents.

In summary, more than three-quarters of buyers feel the salesperson should have at least some idea of what their budget is. However, be cautious when inquiring about budget.

Four

Prospecting

T he single largest contributing factor to poor sales performance is lack of adequate prospecting and sales-producing activities

FOUR ELEMENTS TO EFFECTIVE COLD CALLING

Need to generate sales leads? Get on the phone and start cold calling. Contrary to what you might hear, cold calling works—if you do it right. Your objective when cold calling is getting the buyer to engage in a meaningful conversation about the benefits of your product or service.

The 4 main elements to an effective cold call include:

1. Introduce yourself—state your name and mention your firm
2. Give them a reason to listen—tell the buyer what is in it for him
3. Make a referral statement—gain credibility by referencing something in common
4. Ask for more time to explain your product or service—ask for the next step

HANDLING VOICEMAIL WHEN COLD CALLING

Clearly the first challenge when cold calling is getting someone to answer the phone. Voicemail makes this difficult. Nevertheless, you can increase the likelihood that you will get a return call, or that your subsequent attempts to reach the buyer will be successful.

In our recent survey about selling into the B2B space, we asked buyers what they want to hear in a voicemail message that would motivate them to call back—see chart below.

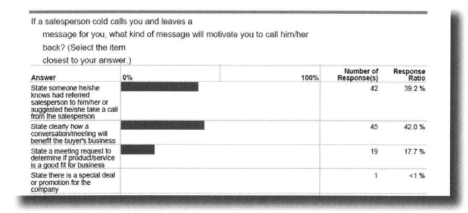

If a salesperson cold calls you and leaves a message for you, what kind of message will motivate you to call him/her back? (Select the item closest to your answer.)

Answer	0%	100%	Number of Response(s)	Response Ratio
State someone he/she knows had referred salesperson to him/her or suggested he/she take a call from the salesperson			42	39.2 %
State clearly how a conversation/meeting will benefit the buyer's business			45	42.0 %
State a meeting request to determine if product/service is a good fit for business			19	17.7 %
State there is a special deal or promotion for the company			1	<1 %

The message that you leave for them has to clearly state the benefit the customer will receive if he talks to you—this is the WIFM...what is in it for me. A close second is name-dropping—referring to the fact that someone the buyer knows and respects is doing business with you and suggested you call. Combine the two and you will significantly increase the probability of a call back.

An example—"Hi Mr. Baker, my name is John Smith and my firm, XYZ Company, has a consistent track-record of reducing shipping costs for companies like yours. Bill Jones (a friend of Mr. Baker) has been using our services and he suggested I give you a call. He thought you would also benefit from what we do. In just a few minutes I can tell you how we do it. Please give me a call back at 555-5555. If I don't hear back from you, I will reach out again in a few days. Once again, this is John Smith and my number is 555-5555. Thanks and have a great day."

This message, which can be delivered in less than 30 seconds, offers the "WIFM" in the first sentence and then backs it up with mentioning the referral source. It communicates a requested action and also states that the caller won't give up if there is no return call.

DELIVERING A SUCCINCT COLD CALL

What happens when you get lucky and get someone to answer the phone? Your script becomes only slightly different. In our survey, we asked buyers what they want to hear that will motivate them to set up an appointment with a salesperson that cold called them—see chart below.

If a salesperson cold calls you and reaches you live, what do you have to hear that will result in you setting up a face-to-face meeting with that salesperson? (Select the item closest to your answer.)

Answer	0%	100%	Number of Response(s)	Response Ratio
Some information that suggests there's something in it for me			19	17.7 %
That someone the buyer knows referred the salesperson			14	13.0 %
The caller is doing business with someone I know and respect			38	35.5 %
Without small-talk, immediately state how a meeting will benefit me			36	33.6 %

Mentioning a referral name and getting straight to the benefit remain the two most important elements. Avoid small talk about how your day is going or what is going on with the weather. The person you are calling doesn't know you and likely won't be interested in having a casual conversation with you. So, get right to the point.

An example—"Hi Mr. Baker, my name is John Smith and my firm, XYZ Company, has a consistent track-record of reducing shipping costs for companies like yours. Bill Jones (a friend of Mr. Baker) has been using our services and he suggested I give you a call because he thought you'd also benefit from what we do. Do you have just a couple of minutes that I can quickly share with you how we do it?"

This statement can be delivered in about 15-20 seconds. It immediately states the benefit and quickly communicates a compelling referral statement. Delivering this kind of opening statement in a cold call will likely result in a "yes" after asking the customer for a couple of minutes to communicate how you deliver your benefits.

Once you get the buyer's attention and agreement to listen, be prepared to communicate succinctly the 2-3 things your company does to achieve the benefit you stated—the WIFM for the customer. When cold calling, have your full script ready to deliver and don't stop your preparation after the opening statement.

Once you have communicated the 2-3 things to achieve the end result for your buyer, pause and do a trial close (more on trial closing in a later chapter).

Cold calling isn't dead, and can actually be very effective for lead generation. Preparing your scripts ahead of time is crucial. Be ready to state how the buyer will benefit and whenever possible, drop some names. Saying you were referred by someone the buyer knows will help attest to your credibility. Stating that you are doing business with other respected firms will continue to boost the buyer's confidence in you. Preparing your scripts and following the 4 elements to effective cold calling will significantly increase your probability of getting into a meaningful discussion with a prospect.

HOW TO QUALIFY YOUR BUYER

Nearly every time you read about the top traits of successful salespeople, you will find a section about qualifying buyers. In sales, the buyer is not the only one who should be making a decision. The salesperson has to decide how much time and energy he is willing to commit to pursue the buyer. Too much time invested in an unqualified buyer prevents the salesperson from working with the right buyers to achieve his goals.

Here is a very sound method for qualifying buyers—the BARTS method—which includes 5 criteria to help you decide if a sales opportunity is worth pursuing.

DOES THE BUYER HAVE THE BUDGET?

It is often challenging to ascertain the buyer's budget. However, our research suggests that buyers are generally comfortable revealing information about their budget. When we asked decision-makers how comfortable they are revealing information about their budgets, nearly 80% indicated they were very or somewhat comfortable.

How comfortable are you telling a salesperson what your budget is for a certain product or service? (Select the item closest to your answer.)

Answer	0% 100%	Number of Response(s)	Response Ratio
Very comfortable - he/she should know what my budget is		29	27.1 %
Somewhat comfortable - he/she should have an idea but don't want to reveal any specific numbers		54	50.4 %
Somewhat uncomfortable - don't want to be too informative about my budget for fear it will be used to sell me more than what I need		14	13.0 %
Very uncomfortable - he/she shouldn't know what I am willing to spend		9	8.4 %
No Response(s)		1	<1 %
	Totals	107	100%

If a buyer fails to give you any indication of his budget, a follow up question like this might help:

*"Based on what we've discussed, the investment for the right solu-
tion could be in the $5,000 to $10,000 range. How does that fit within
your budget?"*

This question will often reveal some information about the budget.
The buyer might say, "That is way out of my league" or "that sounds
about what I was thinking". At that point, you will have much better idea
about whether your buyer meets the "budget" criteria.

DOES THE BUYER HAVE THE AUTHORITY?

A top sales performer needs to determine who has the authority to make
the deal—the individual that has the authority to "sign the check". If you
are investing your time with someone other than the decision-maker, you
run the risk of becoming an inanimate object in the eyes of the decision-
maker. After all, unless you get direct exposure and interaction with the
decision-maker during the sales process, how can you develop a relationship, understand his emotional needs, and get into alignment with what
he wants to accomplish? It is simply impossible.

If you cannot get direct exposure and interaction with the decision-
maker, the salesperson should walk away. Not doing so sets the salesperson
up to invest a lot of time and energy without much to show for it in the end.

IS THE REVENUE YOU WILL GENERATE WORTH YOUR TIME?

A good salesperson assesses the revenue potential of any given buyer
early in the sales process and has to make a decision about whether it is
worth the pursuit.

Let's say your average sale is $5,000 over the first 12 months of a
project. Based on the conversations you are having about the needs of
your buyer, you determine that the first year revenue likely won't exceed
$2,000. If you feel the "customer lifetime value" (CLV) is $20,000 over
the first 4 years, you might determine this to be a qualified buyer. On the
contrary, if it appears that your initial project will be a one-time event with
little to no future revenue potential, you might determine that this deal
doesn't deserve the time and energy you'd have to put into it to close the
sale. You might be better off pursuing another qualified buyer.

WHAT IS THE BUYER'S TIMEFRAME FOR MAKING A DECISION?

How frustrating would it be for you to invest hours into a sale only to find out the buyer won't be making a decision for 6 months? That is what can happen if you fail to establish timing early in the sales process.

This is not to say you that should ignore the buyer and move on to a better qualified prospect. If the sales opportunity meets all the other BARTS criteria, it should go into your lead nurturing process. Remember, only a small fraction of your target market is in the buying mode at any given time.

Due to the complexity of some products and services, the buying cycle might be months or even years in the making. Don't give up on an otherwise qualified buyer. Nurture that buyer through the sales process so that you can make your numbers today, tomorrow, and for the foreseeable future.

DOES THE SOLUTION ADD VALUE?

As I have stated many times, never sell something to a buyer that doesn't truly add value or solve a problem. If you are selling security systems but the buyer's greatest need is improving quality of his manufacturing process, this may not be a qualified buyer. Sure, this buyer may use a security system but you are doing him an injustice if you try to sell him a product/service that doesn't truly address his objectives.

Determine early on if the products and services you offer are what the buyer needs to solve his problem or capitalize on his business opportunity. If it's a good match, go for it. If not, it is better to maintain your reputation as a trusted advisor and refer a vendor who you have confidence in that offers what the buyer needs.

In the end, if you have a sales opportunity that 1) has an appropriate budget, 2) the buyer has the authority to make the buying decision, 3) the revenue you will generate is worth your time and energy, 4) a decision will be made in a timely way, and 5) the solution you are offering adds value, what more could you want? Invest the time and energy with your buyer.

4 STEP PLAN TO DEVELOP A SALES PIPELINE

STEP 1—ARE YOU HANGING OUT WHERE YOUR QUALIFIED PROSPECTS ARE HANGING OUT?

Whether you are networking physically (in-person) or virtually (online), are you networking with qualified prospects—your target market? I have seen too many people networking with groups (in-person and online) where there are too few of their targeted prospects. If you are trying to connect with CEOs of certain sized companies, but the organization with which you are networking attracts mainly accountants or IT professionals, you should re-examine your involvement. Ask yourself—am I involved in the same organizations as my targeted prospects? If not, find and get involved with the right networking groups.

Joining LinkedIn groups is the online version of networking. Are you a member of the best groups that align with your target market? If your answer is "yes", then are you providing original and compelling content in those groups, answering member questions, and being a valuable source within the group? If not, you need to re-examine the group and how you are adding value to it.

STEP 2—DO YOU HAVE A TARGETED PROSPECT LIST?

The best sales professionals always have a list of prospects they want to meet. If you don't, you run the risk of waiting for the next lead to fall into your lap—not exactly an ideal way to make your quota. Depending on the size of your average sale and how many sales you need to make in a given period of time, your prospect list may have as few as 10 or more than 100. The important thing is to have a prospect list.

Here are three ways to develop a prospect list...

- Go to Sales Genie, InfoUSA or one of the other online business information sites. Input your criteria and purchase a list of prospects that align with your target market. The investment isn't much when you consider the potential sales.

- Scan through member lists of business and trade organizations, and pick out those who appear to be aligned with your target market.
- Scan through phone books and newspapers to identify prospect companies. Make sure to be observant when you are driving around and make note of the names on doors when you are in office buildings or simply jot down names of companies that you come across.

Now that you have a list names and companies you want to meet, are you actively working it every day? When you are networking with other individuals, are you reviewing your prospect list with them? When you are meeting with existing clients, are you asking them if they know anyone on your prospect list and can be a reference? Are you searching LinkedIn for people with whom you are connected with to see if they are connected to someone on your prospect list?

Once you exhaust your efforts to connect with prospects through your current networking activities, begin contacting the remaining prospects on your list (more on cold calling at the beginning of this chapter).

STEP 3—ARE YOU CAPTURING EMAIL ADDRESSES?
At every opportunity, capture a prospect's email address. Don't become another annoying "spammer", but rather use contact information with care. When you meet a new prospect, send him a "thank you" note, article, or resource. These ways of follow up will set you apart from the rest. Go further by sending a link to your last newsletter and ask permission to add him to your email database. If you behave like you respect the prospect's time and privacy, you will likely get a warm reception.

In a recent survey, buyers reported email as their most preferred way to receive information about products and services. Use your email database to keep your prospects informed and to nurture your qualified leads through the buying funnel.

STEP 4—ARE YOU PRE-QUALIFYING YOUR LEADS?
Once you obtain enough information about your prospect, you can qualify the lead. The last article covered the "BARTS" method, here's a recap...

B—Does the buyer have the Budget?
A—Does the buyer have the Authority?
R—Is the Revenue you will generate worth your time?
T—What is the buyer's Timeframe for making a decision?
S—Does the Solution add value?

If your prospect meets the "BARTS" criteria, they are worthy of the time that you will spend nurturing them through the buying funnel. If they don't qualify, don't invest too much time until they do.

NETWORKING TECHNIQUES THAT WORK

Business networking, whether online or in-person is a very powerful way to increase your brand awareness and credibility, especially if you are in the business of selling and marketing to other businesses. Besides knowing your business and your competitive advantages, it is important to set goals to achieve through business networking.

When thinking about how business networking fits within your overall marketing plans, ask yourself these questions...

How many people do I want to meet?
How many leads do I want to generate?
How much of my sales plan should be achieved via business networking?

The answers to the above questions will allow you to determine which networking activities and events you should get involved with and how much time you should spend with them. Beyond setting your goals, here are six proven methods that should be an important part of your networking marketing plan.

1. NETWORK IN A TARGET RICH ENVIRONMENT & STAND OUT FROM THE CROWD

Know what kinds of people you want to meet and find the organizations and activities in which those people are involved. Don't go to networking events unless your target market will also be there or you are sub-optimizing your time.

Get involved! Instead of being just another face in the crowd, seek a leadership position or get involved by volunteering. If you don't stand out and work hard on having competitive advantage, try something different because business networking may not be the right fit for you.

2. GIVERS GAIN—HELP OTHERS AND YOU WILL BE HELPING YOURSELF

The old saying "givers gain" means that you should first give and then you will gain from your giving. Call it "the right thing to do" or karma, but this old adage holds true in business networking. Focus first on how you can help others make the connections they want to make. When you meet someone, ask them, "Who are you looking to meet?" or "What kinds of businesses do you want to connect with?" You will become known as a master networker and people will seek you out which will only enhance your personal reputation and your company's brand.

3. BE PREPARED—ELEVATOR PITCH AND GOOD OPEN ENDED QUESTION

Get your "elevator pitch" or Unique Selling Proposition (USP) ready so it rolls off of your tongue as easily as your name does. When someone asks you what you do, you want to be able to articulate your USP with confidence and ease. This is extremely important. For more on creating a USP, refer to the Basic Marketing chapter.

Be ready with a good open-ended question when you meet someone. A question like "Who are you looking to meet?" or "What does your firm do and how might I be able to help you connect with the people you are seeking?" Questions like these will get the other person talking. Remember—givers gain!

4. GOOD FOLLOW UP AFTER MEETING SOMEONE

If you make a good connection, follow up with a kind email or handwritten note expressing gratitude for his/her time. It will make you memorable. Humility and gratitude are traits of every successful sales professional.

Don't just add the person to your email database so they begin getting your unsolicited emails. Instead, in your follow-up email or note, let them know that you will include them in your newsletters and that you hope he/she finds them valuable but can unsubscribe if not. Ask for feedback and advice about your information—that is a sign that you respect the other person's opinion.

At the next networking event, seek out that person just to say hello and express appreciation for making a connection.

5. DON'T SELL AT NETWORKING EVENTS

We have all been to gatherings where one person is always talking or bragging about themselves and is in general being self-centered. They are clearly there only to achieve their own personal objectives with little regard for anyone else's. Don't be that person. You should not sell at networking events—you are there simply to increase your brand awareness, make connections, and help others to make their connections. Your selling activity should take place elsewhere.

6. USE LINKEDIN

LinkedIn is the place for online business networking. It is upscale and easy to use. Make sure your profile is complete and accurately reflects your USP and what you do. Seek out the people you are connected to that might be able to introduce you to the people you want to meet. For more information on using LinkedIn, refer to the Basic Marketing chapter.

In summary, business networking can have a positive impact on your sales success. It can also be a big waste of time. Be prepared, be special, be in the right places, and help others. If you do these things, you become someone well respected within the business community.

HOW TO EVALUATE AND IDENTIFY THE DIFFERENT BUYER TYPES

Do you know who your buyers are? Do you realize how many buyers you have within the same account? The larger the account, the more buyers you will need to communicate with. Buyer types were briefly discussed in the Basic Sales chapter, but here I will explore the four types a bit further and provide ways that you can effectively communicate with them.

As in most areas of our lives, it is critical that our communication appeals directly to the emotional and practical elements of others. Let's admit that even the most practical of us makes decisions based on emotions. These emotions are driven by the two reasons people buy—gain and pain.

When thinking about your different buyers, explore the following questions:

What are the main problems this buyer experiences?
What are the main things that would make the buyer's situation better?
What is important to this buyer relative to deciding on a solution?
What appears unimportant to this buyer?

In sales, like marketing, it is absolutely critical to fully understand the answers to these questions. By having these answers, you can develop marketing messages with features and benefit statements that appeal directly to your buyer. They also help you effectively differentiate yourself and overcome objections.

Here are the four key buyer types…

The "user" buyer—This is the person who will actually use your product or service, or who will be the main person interacting with your company/product/service. This person chooses you to help them get their job done and is asking, "will this product or service solve my problems and needs?"

The "technical" buyer—This person is responsible for making sure proposed solutions meet certain quality standards for the organization.

They give technical approval and ensure the solution meets specifications and requirements. The solution has to integrate easily and effectively with other products, services, and systems within the organization.

The "economic/strategic" buyer—This person writes the check and approves the investment. This buyer is usually the main decision-maker and will want to know what the return on investment will be.

The "inside coach"—This person is a connection within the company, most likely a trusted advisor to the "economic/strategic" buyer. Even though your "inside coach" wants you to get the sale, his reputation is on the line so you must work to understand him just as you do the other buyers.

In summary, understand that you likely have more than one buyer in larger accounts and you need to attend to each of their practical and emotional needs. Knowing their gain opportunities and pain points along with what is and is not important to each of them is important to effectively communicate and position yourself to make the sale.

WAYS TO NURTURE B2B LEADS THROUGH THE BUYING FUNNEL

In the B2B selling world, the higher the price, the longer the sales cycle. Higher priced solutions typically require more research and more people being involved. Elite B2B salespeople are adept at nurturing leads through a long sales cycle. Here are three ways to nurture a qualified lead from initial contact to closing the deal.

1. CHERISH YOUR QUALIFIED PROSPECTS

Significant time and money are usually invested to identify qualified B2B sales leads. If the lead is truly qualified, that prospect may not be ready to buy right now but will probably be ready at some point in the next 2-3 years. It is important that you do not discount or ignore that prospect just because the timing isn't right. Put that prospect in your lead nurturing system (as described below) and continue to strengthen your connection until the time is right to make a sale.

Elite B2B salespeople are disciplined about building and managing a database of qualified leads. It is vital that you document qualified leads and create a system for nurturing those leads through the buying funnel whether you use a CRM (customer relationship management) system like ACT or Salesforce, or a less sophisticated method like an Excel spreadsheet and file folders.

2. CREATE A LIBRARY OF VBR'S (VALID BUSINESS REASONS)

Between voicemail and caller ID, it is hard to make connections with prospects by phone. No one wants to be pestered by "are you ready to buy yet" phone calls. Salespeople who do this become annoying and put themselves in a category with every other pushy salesperson. To separate yourself from the competition and position yourself as a credible expert, you need to create an inventory of VBR's (Valid Business Reasons) to connect with your prospects.

What VBR's you need to have will depend on the needs of your prospects. The first thing to do is identify the problems your prospects have and why they are seeking someone like you. If your firm is selling marketing services, the initial problem might be "what marketing should I be doing to increase sales?" If your firm is selling inventory management systems, the initial problem might be "how do I reduce inventory obsolescence?" Once you identify the main problems that your prospects have, develop a library of reports, demos, articles, etc. that will provide some guidance on how to solve that problem. This helps to address the first phase in the buying funnel—Awareness.

The next phase in the buying funnel is Consideration/Evaluation. What VBR's should you have in this phase? Ideally, you will have some industry reports on how firms have solved problems using solutions similar to those that your firm provides. Additionally, case studies about how your firm has solved the problems are key. Once you' have acknowledged the prospect's problem and demonstrated your industry knowledge and expertise, you want the prospect to understand how your firm can be their ideal solutions provider and solve their problem.

3. USE A LEAD NURTURING SYSTEM

You have got your list of qualified prospects that will be ready to buy at some point in the near future. You also have a library of VBR's that you can use to connect with your prospects throughout the buying funnel. Now you just need to have a system that delivers the VBR's at the right time to the right prospects.

With a good CRM, you can set up and manage the frequency and specifics of how you nurture your prospects. Another emerging method that is growing in popularity is "marketing automation". According to recent reports, about 90% of Fortune 500 companies use marketing automation for lead nurturing where only about 30% of small-to-midsized firms do.

Marketing automation is simply a highly targeted email marketing program. Essentially, you are distributing specific content (VBR's) to specific prospects at a critical time in their buying process. In a recent study about marketing automation, some case studies reported the following...

- PaperStyle.com used marketing automation to follow each bride through the various stages of wedding planning and offer relevant products to match their needs. They achieved a 330% increase in revenue per mailing.

- Online registration service, Acteva, began using marketing automation in order to improve the targeting behind its campaigns and gain a better ROI. They achieved $2 million in incremental revenue, a 350% marketing ROI and 100% annual growth in areas where marketing automation was implemented.
- McAfee increased lead conversion rate by 4 times. Marketing automation enabled McAfee to implement a lead scoring system and create a segmented nurturing program that gave prospects the right information at the right time in the buying process.

Whether you use a CRM tool or implement more sophisticated marketing automation technology, having a system that utilizes your library of VBR's to connect to your qualified prospects is essential. However, it must be with the right frequency at the right time to make you stand out as an industry expert and put you in front of the line when your prospect is ready to buy.

Patience and a good lead nurturing system are critical to achieving great B2B sales results. This success depends on three important things; 1) understanding your prospects' typical problems, 2) building a library of VBR's that educate your buyer through the various stages of the buying funnel, and 3) using a system to deliver the VBR's at the right time to the right people.

HOW TO FIND AND WORK WITH AN INSIDE COACH

Do you want to exponentially increase your chances of getting a face-to-face appointment with a top prospect or closing a big sale? If you answered yes, then you need to get an inside coach. An inside coach is someone on the inside of your prospective company who wants you to get the sale.

An experience I had recently with an inside coach is a perfect example. I had a huge sales opportunity and the prospect was seriously considering five providers including my firm. I needed to separate myself from the competition so I went searching for an inside coach. I found someone who I worked with in the past and we had mutual respect for each other.

The inside coach did not have direct influence over the decision process but she was able to provide me with an in-depth understanding of the company's challenges and strategies. This gave me real insight to integrate into my "pitch".

In my initial meeting with the prospect, I was able to communicate my firm understanding of their challenges. To leverage my knowledge further, I took the Challenger Sales Approach and began explaining how my solution applied in a unique and effective way to solve the company's main problem. Fortunately, I got the sale.

There are necessary criteria an inside coach should have. Not all of them have to apply every time, but the more that do apply, the more impactful the inside coach. Here's what to look for in an inside coach...

- Knowledgeable of the company's requirements
- Credible within the company's organization
- Considers you trustworthy and credible
- Wants you to get the business

SO, HOW DO YOU FIND AN INSIDE COACH?

Start by looking within your current customer base. Perhaps you will find a raving fan among your current customers who may be influential to the decision-maker within the prospective company or who may know someone inside the company that can help you get the sale. Look within your vendors, suppliers, and consultants. You may just find someone who is very knowledgeable about the company and influential to the decision-maker. Go to LinkedIn along with your other social and online networks to find someone inside the prospective company with whom you may be able to contact for information.

If you think hard enough and tap into your contacts and networks, it is not difficult to find an inside coach who has credibility, knowledge, and wants you to get the sale. Find your inside coach and get a direct referral with the decision-maker or at least an insider's perspective of the company. You will have a competitive advantage and a much higher probability of closing the sale.

OUTBOUND MARKETING (TELEMARKETING) TO FILL SALES PIPELINE

Inbound marketing and lead nurturing, using marketing automation platforms (like Hubspot) have proven very effective and many of our clients are seeing remarkable results. However, if you are in sales and have quotas to hit, you need to consider investing some time and money into outbound marketing.

if you think that outbound calling programs are no longer successful then you are wrong. It may be difficult to get the right person on the phone sometimes but you can, and it does work, but only if you do it right. With outbound calling, you can easily predict how many prospects you can generate.

Here are three outbound calling program strategies for sales prospecting as well as some additional advice on how to grow your sales long term.

PREPARATION

Before you begin filling your pipeline with sales prospects, you need to determine who you want to contact. Here are three ways to prepare for your outbound calling program...

1. Buy a list—there are several places like InfoUSA and Sales Genie where you can purchase of list of prospects based on your target market criteria. Realize though, these lists are marginally accurate. A respected source in this space recently estimated the accuracy rate at about 30% regardless of where you purchase the list. Nevertheless, it's a place to start.
2. LinkedIn search—using the advanced search function in LinkedIn, you can generate a list of sales prospects that meet a variety of criteria determined by you—attributes like location, job title, etc. The numbers may not be as large as purchasing a list, but this method produces better quality at a lower cost.
3. Valuable content—obtain or develop some content that is valuable to your target market. This may be an important report about the

industry, a great article, a research study, or something else that the people you are calling find valuable. You will use this to get contact information if you are unsuccessful at getting an appointment

"RIGHT PARTY CALLING"

"Right party calling" is a quick call just to find out who might be your prospective buyer within the target company. These calls are quick and easy to make. Depending on how busy you are, you may decide to outsource this to an individual or call center.

The script might go something like this – "Hi, my name is Neal Lappe and I'm calling to find out who in your company makes decisions about marketing? I'm not selling anything, I'm just curious as to who typically makes those decisions." You won't be 100% successful, but "right party calls" will get you some good information that will make the next step much more productive.

APPOINTMENT SETTING CALLS

These calls are a bit more challenging because the objective is to get an appointment with the person you are calling. Depending on the resources available, you may do this yourself or engage with a firm that specializes in appointment setting calls.

These calls require a good script and more advanced skills. My firm conducted a research study and we asked decision-makers several questions about calls from salespeople. When asked what they would need to hear to set an appointment with a salesperson or to return a sales call, they stated two main things...

1. They want to hear quickly what is in it for them.
2. Secondly, if you can mention someone they know or talk about a well-respected company within the same industry that you work with, you will gain credibility and get their attention.

The script might go something like this – "Hi, my name is Neal Lappe and my firm has developed a unique way of generating sales leads using automated marketing techniques. Joe Schmo (a person known by the person being called) suggested I contact you thinking that your firm might benefit from a program like this. Can I get just a few minutes on your calendar next week to stop by and share a few details?"

The calls you make vs. the appointments you set will be low, but this approach is an effective way to get in front of a qualified buyer. It is a major step towards creating a trusting relationship so that you can do business with him in the future.

CALLS SEEKING ADVICE

Would you like to learn more about what is important to your customers? Most good salespeople would say they do. Calling for advice without selling anything is an effective way to get in front of your target customers. The person receiving the call may be skeptical about your motives, but this method may improve your chances of having a meaningful conversation with a prospective buyer. Worst case, they remain skeptical but feel flattered by your inquiry.

When you make these kinds of calls, be genuine. Don't seek advice unless you are genuinely interested in hearing it. This is not a ploy or a sales pitch; it is a genuine desire to get expert opinion about your product or service. If you can't genuinely ask for advice, then don't attempt it and don't even give the slightest hint that you are making a sales pitch. If you do it right, the prospective buyer will ask you about your product or service and you will be on your way to creating a valuable relationship.

The script might go something like this – "Hi, my name is Neal Lappe and I'm looking for some advice about sales training. I realize that I am asking a big favor of you, but I am trying to improve my service and could use some help. Please know that I have nothing to offer or to sell you – I'm only seeking advice. May I get a few minutes of your time?" When in front of the person, you can begin asking your questions and if they want to use your service or buy your product, you will know.

Whether you are calling to get a contact, set an appointment, or to seek advice, you will have some success and also a good number of "no thank you's". In the case of a "no thank you", do your best to get a name and email address so that you can at least stay in touch with the prospect and provide them valuable information over time. Eventually when that person gets in the buying mode, he will think of you and then you are on your way to making a sale.

In summary, outbound calling remains an effective and predictable way to fill your sales pipeline. Prepare a good script that contains the elements that are important to the buyer and get busy making some calls. Combine this outbound calling program with your automated inbound marketing and lead nurturing plans, and you will undoubtedly have a full pipeline of buyers with whom you can engage to create long lasting relationships.

Five

Rapport

A buyer has to make 4 buying decisions before you can close a deal, and the first one is that they have to buy YOU

STRATEGIES TO SELL YOURSELF

Before your buyer makes a decision to buy anything from you, that buyer has to "buy you" first. The sale won't come if you are not able to make a strong connection with your buyer. Underscoring this challenge, here are some stats that might surprise you...

- You have 7-20 seconds to make a good first impression
- Buyers make up their mind about you in around 30 seconds
- Visual appearance accounts for about 55% of the first impression and what you sound like accounts for another 38%
- Research from a leading sales consulting firm suggests that only 18% of buyers will buy from you if you don't effectively match their personality type

You may have the most amazing selling techniques up your sleeve but if you can't get past the initial impressions, you won't close the deal.

Following are three strategies that will help you sell yourself...

STRATEGY 1—PHYSICAL APPEARANCE

In our sales training research, we asked buyers, "How do you expect salespeople to dress?" Here's what they said...

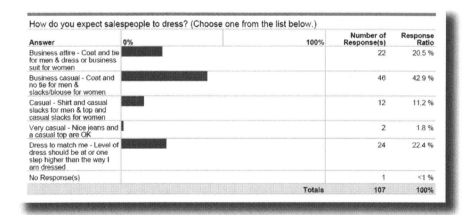

How do you expect salespeople to dress? (Choose one from the list below.)					
Answer	0%		100%	Number of Response(s)	Response Ratio
Business attire - Coat and tie for men & dress or business suit for women				22	20.5 %
Business casual - Coat and no tie for men & slacks/blouse for women				46	42.9 %
Casual - Shirt and casual slacks for men & top and casual slacks for women				12	11.2 %
Very casual - Nice jeans and a casual top are OK				2	1.8 %
Dress to match me - Level of dress should be at or one step higher than the way I am dressed				24	22.4 %
No Response(s)				1	<1 %
			Totals	107	100%

STRATEGY 2—MIRROR & MATCH YOUR BUYER'S PERSONALITY STYLE TO BUILD RAPPORT

As stated throughout this book, you will have a hard time making the sale if you don't build the right rapport and alter your communications style to match that of your buyer. The DISC personality profile is a great way to understand your style and that of your buyer. Read on to the next article for more information on DISC. You can also learn about selling styles in the Basic Sales chapter.

Once you are matching the buyer's style, how best do you build rapport with them? We asked that question in our research for sales training and the data below reveals the most effective rapport building methods.

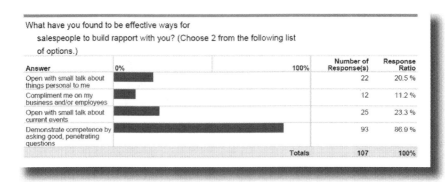

What have you found to be effective ways for salespeople to build rapport with you? (Choose 2 from the following list of options.)				
Answer	0%	100%	**Number of Response(s)**	**Response Ratio**
Open with small talk about things personal to me			22	20.5 %
Compliment me on my business and/or employees			12	11.2 %
Open with small talk about current events			25	23.3 %
Demonstrate competence by asking good, penetrating questions			93	86.9 %
		Totals	**107**	**100%**

STRATEGY 3—PRESENTING YOUR COMPANY

If you have been on the buyer's side of a sales meeting then you know how boring it can be to hear the salesperson go on and on and on about his company. In my experience, this is one of the biggest mistakes salespeople can make. In our sales training research, we asked buyers how much time a salesperson should spend presenting his company. Here's what they said...

If you typically use long Powerpoint presentations or a multitude of sales sheets and marketing materials to show to your customers—stop. Buyers want a meaningful, yet succinct understanding of your company. That is all. If the buyer wants to know more about your company after the presentation, let him ask. Seize this opportunity to learn what is important (and not important) to your buyer.

When a salesperson is presenting information about his/her company, how long should that presentation take? (Select the item closest to your answer.)

Answer	0%	100%	Number of Response(s)	Response Ratio
5 minutes or less			50	46.7 %
5 - 15 minutes			40	37.3 %
15 - 30 minutes			15	14.0 %
More than 30 minutes			1	<1 %
No Response(s)			1	<1 %
		Totals	107	100%

In summary, buyers have to buy you first. They form impressions about you in seconds and these impressions are based on how you look and how you sound—not necessarily what you say. Assess your buyer's personality style and modify your approach to align with his style. Build rapport with good, open-ended questions that communicate a genuine desire to learn how you can help them. And finally, the information you present about your company should be succinct and communicate competitive advantages.

HOW TO MAKE BUYERS LOVE YOU

It's been said over and over—people do business with people they like. Also, the people we like and spend time with are people who are like us and do the things that we like to do. In sales, one of the key ingredients to success is the ability to make the buyer love you, or at least like you more than they like your competition.

A hallmark in the sales training and development business is the DISC profile, which categorizes different communication styles. William Moulton Marston, psychologist and creator of the first functional polygraph, developed the DISC characteristics of behavior after conducting research on human emotions. His theory was converted into a personality assessment tool by industrial psychologist Walter Vernon Clarke.

We encourage everyone whose success depends on interacting with others to complete this short assessment. You can find free versions of the DISC assessment online.

The DISC profile is founded on two dimensions; Assertiveness or Ego Drive (on the vertical y axis), and Responsiveness or Empathy (on the horizontal x axis).

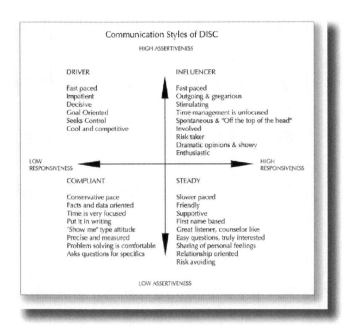

Communication/personality styles are placed into four quadrants based on the individual's assertiveness level (ego drive) and responsiveness level to others (empathy). You can see some of the characteristics of each style in the diagram above.

Historically, about 56% of us fall into the "Influencer" quadrant and another 36% of us are in the "Driver" quadrant. So when we run into a "Compliant" or a "Steady", we really need to adjust our style.

The most difficult person to connect with is the one diagonal to you. For example, a Driver will have the hardest time communicating with a Steady, and a Compliant will have the hardest time communicating with an Influencer. The closer you are to one of the lines or to the middle, the more you are able to adapt to different situations and the more easily you will be able to alter your communication styles to relate to others.

Here's how this relates to sales and getting your buyer to love you; say you are an Influencer as most salespeople are and you are trying to sell to a Compliant individual. Your high level of assertiveness compared to that of your buyer might leave them thinking that you are just another pushy salesperson and they, in turn, will become evasive you will also need to be empathetic, as your compliant buyer normally has a low level of empathy. You don't want your buyer to think you are wasting his time with small talk or non-specific things.

It's important to quickly assess your buyer's communication/personality style—Is your buyer assertive, action-oriented, or dominant? If so, your buyer is probably on the high side of the DISC matrix. Is your buyer friendly, open, gregarious, high energy? If so, your buyer is probably on the right side of the matrix. Is your buyer oriented toward facts or feelings? If more factual, he is on the left side of the matrix. Is your buyer fast or slow paced? If fast paced, he is probably on the high side of the matrix.

Here are some additional tips for altering your style to get your buyer to love you...

- If your DISC profile has you on the high side of the matrix and your buyer is on the low side, you probably need to slow the pace and be less assertive.

- If your profile has you on the left side of the matrix and your buyer is on the right side, you will need to communicate in more creative, conceptual ways; and be friendlier, gregarious, and express more interest in the individual.

Again, people do business with people they like. By quickly assessing your buyer's DISC style and altering your own to align with your buyer, you will be able to relate more easily and effectively with your buyer to ultimately create a stronger personality connection.

5 STEPS TO CONNECTING WITH YOUR BUYERS

Why is it that most people's guard goes up when approached by a sales-person? We are normal people just like you! The reality is that salespeople have a bad rep. This comes from many years of salespeople trying to sell you things you don't really need or want. Here are five easy steps to get beyond the "salesperson stigma"...

At your first meeting with your buyer, follow these steps...

STEP 1—GIVE A COMPLIMENT

Personal affirmation and high self-esteem is something we all desire to have. The better we feel about ourselves, the happier we are. Take the time to make your buyer feel good by giving an honest compliment. Don't tell them how nice the fish on the wall is or how attractive the office looks. It's important to be sincere. Perhaps the receptionist was really helpful or the business has been successful for many years. Saying something like, "I am really impressed by how quickly your business has grown over all these years. It truly says something about the quality of your people." Or you could try, "Your receptionist was remarkably professional. That really gives visitors a great first impression." A sincere compliment like this will likely be positively received by your buyer.

STEP 2—BRING A GIFT

The "Law of Reciprocity" means to give and take mutually; to return in kind or even in another kind or degree. When you give a gift, your buyer's psyche goes to work and he likely feels a need to reciprocate. That reciprocation most often comes in the form of his time, attention and engagement with you. When you give a gift, you begin to break down that resistance or "salesperson stigma" because the buyer wants to return the favor. Don't give the buyer something with your logo on it—you can do that later. A logo gift from your company will make you look like every other salesperson. Give something of value –candy, a gift card to a coffee shop, a lottery ticket, etc. Your customer will appreciate the sincere gesture and you will start to create a good relationship.

Many salespeople in our sales training classes feel some discomfort about giving a gift. That is understandable and I also used to feel that way. These days when I bring a gift, I will say something like "my mother always taught me to bring a gift when I am invited over to someone's place."

STEP 3—BE A SOURCE OF VALUABLE INFORMATION

Your goal should be to separate yourself from your competitors and make a solid connection with your buyer. One of the ways you achieve that is to be a source of valuable information. How do you do that? Bring an article or bring information about your customer's competition that he/she may not already know about. If you are seeing someone in the technology field, bring a recent article or study about technology. If you are seeing someone in the marketing area, bring a good article about that topic. Presented in the right way, your buyer will appreciate your thoughtfulness and value your information. This will position you above your competition, make you look like a knowledgeable person, and further connect you with your buyer.

STEP 4—HAVE AN EXHIBIT

Most people like seeing their name in lights. It is another way of getting personal affirmation. Always have a binder, file folder or some other item that has the customer's name on it. Make it look professional. Print off a copy of the customer's website home page and slide it into a binder cover or adhere it to a file folder. Whether it is the binder or file folder or some other container, use it to keep all the relevant information about that buyer. When your buyer sees it, he will likely think two things: 1) "I see my name and that gives me a feeling of importance" and 2) "this salesperson has obviously done some preparation". Both thoughts will build your connection.

STEP 5—MAKE A REFERENCE

Let's say you are calling on a trucking company that wants to implement a new system of some type. Making a statement like, "I'm really interested in learning more about what you are trying to achieve here. We recently did a project where we implemented a customer tracking system for a courier service and it worked great for them. Some of what we learned on that project might be helpful with what you are trying to achieve." A statement like this drives your credibility level to new heights, and likely separates you from your competition.

In summary, by giving compliments, bringing gifts, being a source of good information, having exhibits and making good reference statements, you will shorten the time it takes to build credibility and a connection with your buyer. This sets you above your competition and overcomes the "sales stigma". Never ever lie to a buyer or be insincere—smart people will see through that in a second. Sometimes it takes a little extra work to come up with relevant information or make a sincere compliment, but the investment will pay off in your favor.

Six

Uncovering Pain & Gain

Buyers buy for two reasons and two reasons only – to avoid pain or solve a problem, and to gain something that makes their life better. If you can effectively uncover the pain and gain, you will sell a lot.

LISTENING –THE MOST IMPORTANT SKILL

Buyers want to talk to salespeople who can listen and interpret what is being said. Buyers get impatient when the salesperson is talking too much. In fact, a talkative salesperson is the one that buyers claim annoys them the most.

In our own research on how buyers interact with salespeople, we found that the top trait valued most by buyers is when a salesperson "actively listens to me". See chart below for results of the top 3 most valued traits.

What are the top 3 most valued traits in a
salesperson? (Choose 3 from the following list of options.)

Answer	0%	100%	Number of Response(s)	Response Ratio
Punctual, on-time			27	25.2 %
Dresses well			0	0.0 %
Speaks well			27	25.2 %
Takes notes			11	10.2 %
Asks good questions			74	69.1 %
Actively listens to me			86	80.3 %
Tells about his/her firm			5	4.6 %
Good problem solver			52	48.5 %
Asks for the sale			4	3.7 %
Experience in my industry			21	19.6 %
Other			10	9.3 %
		Totals	107	100%

We know from studies and from experience that buyers have to buy you first. They decide before anything else whether or not they want to work with YOU. Only after that do they decide whether they want to buy your company and eventually, your products or services.

How do you make a connection with your buyer and separate your-self from your competition? In our research, we asked that question and learned that the second most important ability is asking good questions and listening closely. See chart below for the foremost things that can separate you from your competition.

What things are most effective at separating a salesperson from his/her peers? (Choose 2 from the following list of options.)			Number of Response(s)	Response Ratio
Answer	0%	100%		
Ask penetrating questions and listens closely			51	48.1 %
Understanding my business			45	42.4 %
Showing me successful and relevant case studies			8	7.5 %
Showing credibility and sincerity			18	16.9 %
Knowledge of his/her product knowledge			21	19.8 %
Demonstrates ability to solve my problem			68	64.1 %
		Totals	106	100%

Clearly, listening skills is a trait that buyers value highly. How do you develop this valued skill? Here are four things that you should practice in order to become a better listener.

1. ASK A LOT OF QUESTIONS
Do you ever wonder why a child will ask "why" after every statement? Developing a natural curiosity is a great way to put you in a position to listen. I am certainly not suggesting that you ask "why" after every statement a buyer makes. Instead, ask broad but relevant open-ended questions to get your buyer talking. Only then, can you practice these three things to become a better listener.

2. CLEAR YOUR MIND AND FOCUS TOTALLY ON THE BUYER
In a previous chapter, I described how to present your company in a sales type setting. That article encouraged you to be succinct so that you can get to the more important topics – learning about your buyer and how you might be able to support him in achieving his objectives.

Buyers buy for only two reasons—to gain something or to avoid a pain. By focusing totally on the buyer's perspective and listening, you will understand their point of view (gain or pain) before ever thinking about your product or service.

3. TAKE NOTES
Throughout my lengthy career in business, I can remember a handful of instances that left an indelible mark in my mind. One in particular

happened very early in my career. I was called into the VP's office to talk one-on-one about a project. In those days, this man was like God to me. I walked into the room and he just stared at me for an uncomfortable few seconds and suddenly said, "Do not ever walk into this office again without something to take notes on." To this day, I always have a pen and paper with me no matter what meeting I go into.

Taking notes has tremendous benefits in a sales situation. When you are working hard to gain critical information from your buyer, you want to make sure that you get it right and really capture the nuances. It's extremely valuable having notes to refer to when developing a proposal.

I almost always ask permission to takes notes before doing so. You show your respect for the buyer and it gets him used to saying "yes", which I hope he will continue to do all of the way through the process until I ask for the sale.

4. PRACTICE "ACTIVE LISTENING"

What is "active listening"? It is when you give the buyer feedback after hearing what they have to say. For example, the following are active listening statements you can make after the buyer has answered a question...

1. "What I think I heard you say is ...."
2. "What I am hearing is ...."
3. "It sounds like you are concerned about ...."

Active listening statements like these show your buyer that you hear what he is saying. Additionally, the buyer will often add more information or clarify what he wanted to say. These added details are generally rich with information about the buyer's pain and gain points.

Getting good at active listening will help you better connect with your buyer and allow them to share details they may not be so willing to share with your competition.

In summary, buyers value salespeople who ask great questions and listen well. To become a better listener, ask broad but relevant questions that focus totally on the buyer. Always take notes and use your active listening skills. Keep practicing these techniques and you will gain the respect of your buyer while obtaining valuable information to help you close the deal.

OPENING QUESTION

How can you get your buyer to tell you his biggest challenges and greatest fears? Asking good questions and actively listening are very important skills and they are also some of the most difficult to master. This, combined with the importance of rapport building in any formal sales meeting creates major challenges to overcome in your quest to get your buyer to be open and forthright.

A good opening question or "conversation starter" is critical to getting off on the right foot. It has three important benefits...

1. It gets the buyer talking about something important to him or her
2. It begins to build a good rapport between you and the buyer
3. It separates you from other salespeople

If you can successfully ask a good opening question when you meet your buyer, you will begin laying the foundation to developing a strong relationship and hopefully making a sale. Some research up front, along with a comfortable delivery will lead to success.

RESEARCH TO IDENTIFY A TOPIC FOR YOUR OPENING QUESTION

First, you need to research your buyer. Online resources including LinkedIn and Facebook are often the best methods. Go to LinkedIn and find a common connection and ask that connection questions regarding the buyer (this tactic alone is grossly under-utilized).

Dig in and find your common interests whether they be technical, professional, business, or personal. If you, are able to find something the two of you have in common, you will be all the better for it. If not, identify a topic of interest to your buyer that meets the following criteria:

1. It will enhance the buyer's self-esteem
2. It is a topic that can be discussed in depth if necessary and appropriate
3. It is something in which you are interested in or curious about

Once you have identified a good topic, the next step is to formulate the question.

FORMING AND DELIVERING YOUR OPENING QUESTION

Let's say, in your research you learned the following things about your buyer...

1. She has traveled frequently to Europe
2. She dresses fashionably
3. She received a degree in engineering at University of VA
4. She volunteers at a shelter for the homeless and indigent
5. She mentors other female engineers early in their careers

Following are some examples of good opening questions based on what you know about this buyer...

1. *"While preparing for this meeting, I learned that you actively volunteer at the Main Street homeless shelter. I've volunteered at XYZ shelter. What caused you to start volunteering and what is it like at that shelter?"*
2. *"While preparing for this meeting, I learned that you helped start a program for mentoring female engineers early in their careers. That is a great contribution! What prompted you to start mentoring and how has it been working?"*

Notice that I did not include examples of European travel, fashion, or UVA. This is because those topics don't lend themselves to business. They don't have the self-esteem impact of altruism or mentoring and may not generate as much discussion.

If your opening question is a good one, then your buyer will have a lot to say and that will be your starting point in acquiring the information you will need to create a strong relationship and to ultimately make the sale.

Don't get impatient and end rapport building prematurely. Remember, the rapport and relationship building phases are over when the buyer decides that they are over. If you have a talker that appears to have the energy to go on forever, a good question to help you refocus the meeting might be something like, "That is really interesting. By the way, how are we doing with your time?"

In summary, conduct proper research on your buyer and formulate a good opening question that will appeal to the interests and emotions of your buyer. This is the first step to begin building a relationship and will enable you to learn as much as you can learn to help you determine if they are a good customer for you.

USING 4 TYPES OF QUESTIONS TO UNCOVER PROBLEMS AND FIND VALUE

I read a sales book recently that has had a major impact on my methods for asking questions in selling situations. The book is *Spin Selling* by Neil Rackham. Neil spent many years conducting a major research project to determine the optimal selling approach for large sales situations. If you are in the B2B selling arena, this book is a must read.

My biggest take-away from the book was the four types of questions for a sales situation and the sequence in which you should ask them. Here, I will provide a high-level summary of the four types of questions that will lead to bigger sales.

The image below illustrates the four types of question and the sequence in which they should be asked. To give specific examples to illustrate how to apply these principles, I will provide examples based on selling sales training and process development services.

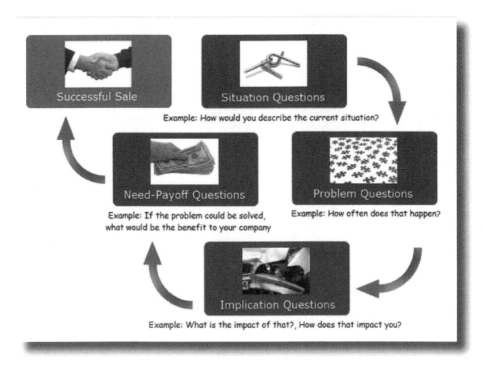

Successful Sale

Situation Questions

Example: How would you describe the current situation?

Need-Payoff Questions

Example: If the problem could be solved, what would be the benefit to your company

Problem Questions

Example: How often does that happen?

Implication Questions

Example: What is the impact of that?, How does that impact you?

SITUATION QUESTIONS

Situation questions should be asked at the beginning of a sales call once you have established rapport and the buyer is talking freely. These questions are meant to give you a sense for what the buyer is currently doing. Here are some examples…

> *"How are you training your sales staff currently?"*
> *"How are you investing in the continued development of your sales team?"*
> *"What sales training programs have your salespeople completed?"*

Questions of this nature get the buyer talking about what he is doing relative to the services you are selling.

PROBLEM QUESTIONS

Problem questions should come next and are designed to uncover "pain points" or problems that the buyer is facing. Following the Situation questions, here are some examples of Problem questions…

1. *"What improvements have you seen in the performance of your salespeople since their training?"*
2. *"How well are you achieving your sales goals?"*
3. *"How consistent are the sales performance levels of your individual salespeople?"*

These questions will allow you to uncover what might be working and also get a better understand of what is not working. They help you determine what problems need to be solved and what pain the buyer is currently experiencing. It is important for me to emphasize that I never suggest a salesperson sell something to a buyer unless it will truly add value and solve a real problem. If, after asking a series of good Problem questions, you are not able to uncover a problem, congratulate the buyer and move onto to a better sales opportunity.

IMPLICATION QUESTIONS

While Situation and Problem questions are common, Implication questions are somewhat unique. These questions are meant to dig a little deeper into the problems you have discovered and should bring forth the consequences or impact of those problems. Here are some examples of Implication questions...

1. *"How has the lack of improvement in sales performance affected overall company performance and profitability?"*
2. *"What impact has the lower sales performance had on the morale and retention of your salespeople?'*
3. *"What impact has not meeting your sales goals had on you personally?"*

Implication questions will take the problems and make them very real, very fast. Implication questions need to be prepared ahead of time. In fact, I recommend you make a list of the 10 most relevant Implication questions associated with your product or service. Implication questions require you to think fast so it is imperative to prepare if you want success.

NEED-PAYOFF QUESTIONS

You have likely heard sales leaders talk about selling and pricing based on value. Need-Payoff questions are essential to determining the value of the solutions you have for the buyer's problems. If you are able to show there will be a strong ROI from your solutions, the buyer will be very likely to invest. Here are some examples...

*   *"If you saw just a 10% increase in sales performance from your sales team, what impact will that have on profitability?"*
*   *"If your salespeople were more consistent at achieving your sales commissions and bonuses, what impact would that have on salesperson retention?"*

- *"If you didn't have to invest so much time coaching your lesser performers, how could you use that extra time to benefit overall company performance?"*

In essence, Need-Payoff questions position the buyer to tell you how your product or service will benefit them, rather than you having to explain it all yourself. Wouldn't it be great to have your buyer sell himself? That is what Implication questions are designed to do.

In summary, the sequence of asking these 4 types of questions is meant to 1) understand the current situation, 2) uncover the problems and pain points from the current situation, 3) enable the buyer to understand the impact of the problems, and 4) help the customer see the value in your solutions. If you have asked the right questions and followed the sequence, your buyer will be ready to buy.

NEGOTIATING SKILLS CAN IMPROVE SALES

Negotiating is a topic that really fascinates me. It is interesting to see how a person's unique human behavioral elements influence exactly how they negotiate and respond in certain situations. The skills used in negotiations align closely to the selling skills of elite salespeople. B2B salespeople are often put in situations to negotiate the terms of a sale. Negotiating and selling skills are intertwined.

This section describes the three most important elements of successful negotiations and expands on how to use them skills in a selling situation. The three critical elements of negotiation are 1) knowing precisely what you want to achieve, 2) maintaining trust and credibility, and 3) understanding how the other person perceives their world. Here is a deep-dive into each element...

KNOW PRECISELY WHAT YOUR GOAL IS BEFORE NEGOTIATIONS BEGIN

Before you even begin your negotiations or move toward closing the sale, understand precisely what you want to accomplish. You may want to make sure a certain set of terms are included in your agreement. Perhaps you want to sell a certain product or service, or want to achieve a certain profit margin from the sale. You may want to experiment with a new service, or simply move your buyer in a direction that ultimately results in reaching that goal.

Whatever it is you want to accomplish in the negotiation or sales situation, make sure everything you do moves you toward that goal. You may find yourself moving sideways occasionally, but if an action or statement moves you further away from your goal, avoid it.

TRUST AND CREDIBILITY ARE REQUIRED TO BE AN EFFECTIVE NEGOTIATOR

No matter how tough the negotiation is or how hard-hitting the person with whom you are negotiating may be, you must build trust and credibility. Without it, you will make little meaningful progress toward your goal. If the other person is suspicious at all about your motives, it will be very difficult to form a relationship and communicate with sincerity.

Avoid being adversarial, even in tough situations. Kill the other person with respect and kindness. You may even make a comment like, "if I get too aggressive or demanding, please let me know" or "if you feel like I'm being too pushy, tell me because I get so passionate about what we do". These statements increase your credibility, communicate respect, and make you look real.

UNDERSTAND THE OTHER PERSON'S PERSPECTIVE OF THINGS

This is like knowing what cards the other person is holding in a poker game. Knowing what is and isn't important to the other person is crucial to achieving your goal and creating a win-win negotiation. You must understand the other person's perspective on the things that relate to the negotiation.

How do you learn about the other person's perspective? It is important that you ask a lot of profound open ended questions—just like the best salespeople do in a selling situation. Remember, you will learn nothing about the other person's perspective when you are talking. It is only when you ask good questions and listen that you can begin to understand what is and isn't important to them.

In a negotiation situation, you might simply say "I'm interested to know what is most important to you about this situation". Another great way to put yourself in a position to understand them better, may be to say, "I want to make sure this is a win-win situation for both of us, what would make this a win for you?"

Furthermore, let's say that a customer makes a demand that seems unreasonable. Instead of responding with something like, "I don't think that was part of the project", you would ask, "what is it that you are trying to accomplish with that?" The customer responds and you might say "that is interesting, and just so I understand better, why is this important to you?"

In a sales situation, you might ask something like, "what is most important to you in this situation?" or "what criteria will you be using to make a decision about which supplier to use?" Both of these questions will get you a long way toward understanding your buyer's perspective.

Finally, always ask open-ended questions and listen actively and emphatically. This will give you an open door into the mind of the other person. It might also compel the person to be more open and empathetic to what is important to you.

An effective negotiator, just like an elite salesperson, should focus on three important elements. First, realize what you want to accomplish and what is important to you in the situation. Second, kill the other person with kindness and respect. It will be harder for the other person to be tough when you are so kind and respectful. Finally, seek first to understand what is important to them before expressing what is important to you.

4 TOOLS FOR HANDLING OBJECTIONS

You will likely see several different kinds of buyers in your journey to becoming an elite salesperson. Many of these buyers will be different, value different things, think differently, and respond differently to various behaviors. Consequently, no matter how good you are, you will have to deal with buyer objections when trying to sell your product or service. This article describes four important tools to have in your "sales bag" that will help you overcome buyer objections.

TOOL 1—PREDICTING THE OBJECTIONS

If you have been selling your product or service for a while, you probably know the most frequent objections. If you don't, ask one of the more experienced salespeople or someone else who understand the product or service. Thinking about and documenting the most frequent buying objections is a critical tool to successfully overcoming them.

When thinking about common objections, make sure you include the pricing objection. It may not always come up, but it is likely on everyone's mind and something for which you should be prepared.

TOOL 2—PREPARING GOOD MARKETING STATEMENTS

Once you have documented your most frequent sales objections, you need to think about a strong marketing statement related to each objection. Marketing statements have two styles; one communicates why the buyer should buy your product or service, and the other is why the buyer should not buy from a competitor. Here are some examples...

1. Why buy from you – *"Our inventory control system is the only one on the market that provides real time updates. This will reduce labor costs because it prevents your warehouse people from searching for product that doesn't exist."*
2. Why not buy from a competitor – *"Unlike the systems that our competitors sell, our system updates inventory levels in real time, which will reduce your labor costs."*

Think about a good marketing statement associated with each of the objections you identified earlier.

TOOL 3—USING EMPATHY

Buyers are taking some level of risk every time they make a decision to buy a product or service, particularly purchases in the B2B space. A good salesperson should be empathetic to the buyer's challenges and risks. Including empathy when you respond to objections is a way to strengthen your relationship with your buyer and improve the likelihood that you will close the sale.

One of the most effective communication techniques in a sales environment is the use of Feel-Felt-Found (FFF). Here's how FFF works, along with examples...

Step	An example of what you say...	Why is this appropriate?
Step 1: Feel – expressing empathy	"I understand why you would be concerned about the length of time required to implement the system."	You are acknowledging and empathizing with the concern your buyer has expressed—not ignoring it.
Step 2: Felt— making the buyer feel legitimate	"We have had other customers express a similar concern."	You are validating and legitimizing the objection—not minimizing it in any way.
Step 3: Found— giving another reason to buy	"What they found is that once the system is set up and operational, it produced savings at a rate faster than if you implemented a less robust solution."	You are explaining how your solution overcomes the stated objection.

By empathizing with the buyer and legitimizing his objections, you communicate an understanding. Then, completing the FFF cycle with a marketing statement will mitigate the risk and overcome the skepticism.

TOOL 4—TRIAL CLOSING QUESTIONS

Trial closing is not asking for the sale but rather asking how the buyer feels about the issues being discussed. The trial close is an open-ended, opinion-asking question that lets the salesperson know where he is in the sales process. Here are some examples of trial closing questions:

1. What do you think?
2. How do you feel about that?
3. How does this sound to you?
4. How valuable is that to you?
5. How do you feel that would help you?

Asking a good trial closing question often results in the prospect raising an objection. This is not at all a bad thing. Objections help you to understand what is important to the prospect and what impediments there may be to making the sale. Additionally, trial closing questions enable you to see if you have successfully overcome the buyer's objections.

Combining trial closing with FFF looks like this...

1. You ask a trial closing question – *"What do you think about that?"*
2. Buyer raises an objection, and you deploy the FFF method to respond to the objection.
3. After making the marketing statement at the end of the FFF cycle, you ask another trial closing question like "how do you feel that would help you?"
4. The buyer might raise another objection and you repeat the above steps 1-3

You can overcome sales objections like a pro when you implement these four tools. Determine the expected objections, prepare marketing statements, show empathy to the buyer, and ask good trial closing questions to see where you are in the sales process.

IMPORTANCE OF TRIAL CLOSING

The most important thing you can do to improve your sales closing performance is to master "trial closing" techniques. Trial closing achieves two necessary things:

1. It allows you to gauge where you are in the sales process.
2. It lets you know when to ask for the sale.

For example, let's say that you are shopping for a smartphone. You go into the store and the salesperson greets you. She finds out what you are looking for and begins to demo the voice activation feature on one of the smartphone models. When she finishes showing you how the voice activation feature works, she asks "what do you think about this voice activation?" That is a great trial close question.

TRIAL CLOSING QUESTIONS—THE SALESPERSON'S MOST VALUABLE TOOL (MVT)

The trial close is the salesperson's MVT. It's like a thermometer or blood pressure cuff—a critical diagnostic tool used to assess a situation. It assess how the prospect feels about the product or service you are selling.

During your time with a prospect, you should constantly be taking his/her "temperature" to determine if they are cold, warm or hot; and react accordingly.

Without a trial close, a salesperson is lost. Whether or not they learn to trial close will have more impact on their closing ratio than any other skill in their career.

Salespeople should practice trial closing until it becomes an instinctive part of the sales process. Since the number one goal of a professional salesperson is to achieve a 100% close ratio, effective trial closing will get you there faster and easier than any other sales technique.

TRIAL CLOSING AND ASKING FOR THE SALE IS NOT THE SAME

Here is the difference between asking for the sale and trial closing:

Asking for the Sale: *"If I can get you the payment terms you are seeking, will you be ready to buy?"* Clearly this is asking for the ultimate buying decision.

Trial Closing: *"How do you feel about the payment terms?"* You are not asking for the sale, you are asking how the prospect feels about one element of the sale.

WHY IS TRIAL CLOSING SO IMPORTANT?

In my experience as a professional sales consultant and sales trainer, I have seen far too many examples of salespeople talking about their product or service and then asking for the sale. In these cases, most salespeople don't really know where they are in the sales process. When they try to close the deal, there are too many unanswered questions on the part of the buyer and the answer is "no".

The salesperson doesn't like the word "no" and doesn't know how to respond, so he/she walks away with another lost opportunity.

The first reason to trial close is to understand where you are in the sales process so that you know what is important to the buyer and where to take the conversation. Remember the previous example of the thermometer—if you don't take the patient's temperature during the diagnosis and ask about symptoms, then how can you determine what to prescribe? You just cannot make a sound diagnosis or ask for a decision from a buyer if you don't know where you are in the process.

The second reason to trial close is to find out when it is appropriate to ask for the sale.

Knowing when to ask for the sale is much more important than knowing how to ask for the order. I don't believe in hard closing a customer as it is just too uncomfortable. I would rather be a trusted advisor than a hard closer. If you know when to ask for the sale, then how you ask for it will be so much easier.

SOME EXAMPLES OF COMMON TRIAL CLOSING QUESTIONS

I have included some examples of common trial closing questions below. Think about these in terms of how easy they are to ask and how much information you can get from your prospect.

"How do you feel about what we have discussed so far?"
"What do you think about the solution I have shared with you?"
"How does what we have talked about sound to you?"
"Based on what you have heard so far, what are your questions?"
"If you had your way, what changes would you make to the proposal?"

Really easy questions, right?

Remember though, these are all open-ended questions. You need to ask a trial closing question that will get the prospect talking so you can learn where you are in the sales process and know when the time is right to ask for the sale.

HOW BUYERS RESPOND TO TRIAL CLOSING

When you ask a trial closing question, you will likely get one of three types of responses; Cold-as-Ice, I'm-Feeling-It, or Ready-to-Roll. The following information provides some guidance on how to best respond.

Cold as Ice—If you get this type of response to a trial closing question, then it is clear you have not broken through yet and you need to ask a follow up question that immediately captures your prospect's attention. Here is an example...

SALESPERSON: "What do you think about what I have presented so far?"
PROSPECT: "I don't think I would be interested."
SALESPERSON: "I can appreciate that. One other question I have though is how does your company handle transportation delays, which can affect your manufacturing time tables?"

Result: The prospect responds with information and the salesperson asks another open ended question to find out if the prospect is still in a mode of resistance.

I'm Feeling It – If you get this type of response to your trial closing question, you know you are on the right track and are making progress.

It is time to strengthen your story before asking for the sale. Here's an example...

> SALESPERSON: "How do you feel about everything we have talked about so far?"
> PROSPECT: "Everything sounds pretty good so far."
> SALESPERSON: "When we first met you mentioned that your company is having a hard time meeting delivery schedules. Could you tell me a little more about that?"

Result: The prospect responds and the salesperson then discusses another feature that deals with this new element.

Ready-to-Roll – If you get this type of response to your trial closing question, then it is time to ask for the sale. Here's an example...

> SALESPERSON: "How does what we've discussed sound to you?"
> PROSPECT: "It sounds really good. This is what we are looking for."
> SALESPERSON: "Great, what is the next step from your perspective?"
> PROSPECT: "I'd like to get things started."
> SALESPERSON: "Sounds good. All I need is your signature on the order form and we can get things going immediately. "

Trial closing questions are open-ended, opinion-asking questions. They enable you as the salesperson to assess where you are in the sales process and evaluate the readiness of your prospect in order to ask for the sale. The response you get from your trial closing question will let you know what you need to do next. The effective use of trial closing questions will improve your closing ratio more than any other technique you possess.

Seven

Closing

Asking for the sale is one of the hardest skills to master. To become an elite salesperson, you have to know when and how to ask for the sale.

HOW TO GAIN COMMITMENT FROM YOUR BUYER

Failing to get some level of commitment from a buyer before providing a proposal is one of a professional salesperson's biggest mistakes. Many salespeople will ask a buyer, "Would you like me to put a proposal together for you?" Think about it, what buyer would respond "no" to that question? After all, the salesperson ends up doing all the work and providing free consulting to the buyer. Buyers expect, and to some degree, deserve free consulting but the imbalance of time in this scenario is inappropriate.

In my more than 10 years selling services into the B2B space, three strategies have emerged that lead to higher close rates on proposals that my team presented.

FIND THE BUDGET

Think about it—how can you put together a proposal that makes any sense to the buyer unless you have some idea about the buyer's budget? In my experience, buyers are often illusive about their budgets but our research suggests that most buyers are willing to share some information. In fact, when we asked buyers about their willingness to reveal their budget, 77% of buyers responded as "very comfortable" and "somewhat comfortable". Find out more about uncovering the budget in the Basic Sales chapter.

GET A COMMITMENT BEFORE THE PROPOSAL

A common problem with many professional salespeople is that they fail to establish a peer relationship with the buyer. Many salespeople lack confidence and become subservient to the buyer. This should never be the case. Salespeople should respect buyers for the value they bring to their firms and salespeople should create value for the buyer in the way they can solve problems and help the business. In our research, we found that buyers value a salesperson's ability to solve problems more than any other skill. Learning the business, being a trusted advisor, and collaborating with the buyer to solve problems and enhance the business are the things salespeople can do to create an ideal peer relationship.

Elite salespeople get a commitment from the buyer before investing time to develop a customized proposal. How do you get that commitment? Ask the buyer...

> *"If I present a proposal that makes sense to you, achieves the objectives we have agreed to, and fits your budget, what will be your next step?"*

First, this is a great open-ended question and one that will help you understand your buyer's level of commitment to take action. It doesn't put the buyer on the spot or come across as a pressure tactic. You are simply asking about how the buyer will evaluate and make a decision to the solutions you will propose.

The response you get from this question will reveal a lot about how committed the buyer is to take action. Many buyers will respond by saying that they will think about it. In this case, the salesperson's follow up question should be something like...

> *"That is fair. What criteria will you use to evaluate whether or not it's appropriate to move forward with the proposal?"*

Once again, this is another great open-ended question that will reveal more about what the buyer values and what the buyer will do upon receiving your proposal. At this point, a deeper discussion will help you to understand the customer's value drivers and his process for making a decision. This is information you can discuss with the buyer to ensure you are collaborating together, rather than being in a subservient role to the buyer.

OFFER OPTIONS

In our research of buyers, we found that 84% want to be offered options rather than simply one solution. Moreover, 54% of buyers would like to be presented with 3 different options. This makes a lot of sense as most of us would rather choose from options than be told what to do. People don't want to be sold to, but they do want to buy.

When it comes to presenting options, we support the ZOPA principle—Zone of Proposal Agreement. Applying the ZOPA principle, we recommend your proposal includes three options in a Good-Better-Best approach. Presenting Good-Better-Best types of options will likely lead to a higher close ratio and a higher average sale. To learn more about improving your close ratio, read on to the ZOPA article later in this chapter.

Increase the number of times you get a "yes" to your proposals by getting a handle on your buyer's budget. Once you know the budget, get a commitment from the buyer on how he will react to your proposal before you invest the time to develop the proposal. Finally, include 2-3 options in your proposal that make sense for your buyer. Apply these three strategies, and you will increase the number of times you get a "yes".

RECOGNIZING THE BUYER SHIFT

The national sales closing rate is around 27%—WOW. When you think about all of the time and money spent meeting with prospects, studying their situation, and developing proposals, to only convert slightly more than 1 out of 4 is a problem. Clearly, most salespeople are not adept in their closing skills.

Among the top 10 selling skills we teach in our classes, knowing when and how to close the sale is the most difficult of them all. This article focuses on how to recognize the verbal and non-verbal signals that indicate when the buyer is ready to be asked for the sale.

In my experience selling in the B2B environment, there are few buyers who will close themselves—unfortunately. The key is recognizing what we call the "buyer shift". The "buyer shift" generally occurs when the buyer has heard enough about the benefits of your products and services to their business and is ready to take some action.

In most situations, body language and tone of voice are the indicators of the "buyer shift". In fact, body language accounts for the majority of signals. As you and the prospect are discussing benefits, watch how the prospect's body language shifts. Here are some common signs of when the shift does and doesn't take place...

Green Light (this shift has occurred)

- Facial – friendly, smiling, slow head nod, chin stroke, pleasant expression
- Arms – released, relaxed, uncrossed
- Eyes – good eye contact, raised eyebrows, rapid blinking eyes
- Hands – palms open, rubbing hands together, handling your material
- Legs – uncrossed or crossed and towards you
- Body Angle – relaxed, upright and toward you, sitting on edge of chair

Red Light (do not attempt to close yet)

- Facial – tense, rubs eye, furrowed brow, pursed lips, nose/face scratch
- Arms – tense, crossed
- Eyes – raising one eyebrow, looking at watch, glazed over, poor eye contact
- Hands – clasped/clinched, fidgeting with objects, pen tapping, in pockets
- Legs – crossed at ankles, crossed away from you, tapping foot
- Body Angle – slouching, leaning away, turning away from you

In addition to these strong non-verbal signals, there are also verbal signals that indicate the "buyer shift". In many cases the buyer begins making statements that imply mental engagement with you and your product/service. Following are some verbal signals to listen for...

- *Buyer attachment statements*—"this is a good location for the item" or "this all sounds pretty good" or "I can see how this could have an impact on our business" or "if we worked with you, how do things get started?"
- *Buyer repeats a question*—"can you explain once again how this element works?" or "I'd like to learn a little more about this feature."
- *Buyer asks a risk-mitigation question*—"so you said this comes with a guarantee" or "what happens if our initial actions don't work?"

- *Buyer mentions an outside recommendation*—"Bob is working with you guys and he says he's been pleased" or "Linda mentioned that she's been happy with what you have done for her."
- *Buyer communicates unfavorable comments about a competitor*—"we are also talking to XYZ Company, but I'm not sure they are the best choice" or "I am confused about why ABC Company suggested a different approach."
- *Buyer asks for personal details*—"how long have you been with your company?" or "what will your involvement be with implementing this solution?"

When body language and other non-verbal signals indicate engagement and a connection with you, and you begin hearing statements and questions that suggest the buyer is envisioning working with you or your products/services, the "buyer shift" is occurring. At this point, you need to be ready to ask for the sale or at least ask some trial closing questions to uncover any other objections before asking for the sale.

Nearly half of all sales calls end without an attempt to close the sale. Additionally, if you are timid about asking for the sale, you have a 90% chance of losing the sale. You should never ask for the sale until the buyer is ready. So, watch body language and listen for buying statements to determine if the "buyer shift" has occurred. Then and only then, ask for the sale.

WHEN TO ASK FOR THE SALE

Studies by sales organizations have consistently identified the two most difficult selling skills:

1. Asking good, profound questions, and listening intently and actively to buyers
2. Knowing when to ask for the sale, and then actually asking for it

Our research shows that buyers want to explain their gain opportunities and pain points, and salespeople should be talking no more than about 30% of the time—the rest of the time listening intently to what they buyer is saying. Moreover, our research finds that buyers value listening skills, asking good questions, and being a good problem solver as the traits they look for in a salesperson.

On the flip side, what do companies value most in their salespeople? Making sales! To be an effective salesperson, you have to ask for the sale. Studies show that nearly half of sales calls end without an attempt to close the sale. In addition, another study found that the national sales closing rate is only about 27%.

So, how does a salesperson "bridge the gap" between just being a good listener and making the sale? This article will bridge that gap and focus on two things: 1) how to ask your buyer questions so that you know when to ask for the sale, and 2) how to ask for the sale.

Sales conversations can be long or short, straightforward or complicated. You might ask many open ended questions and if you are good, you will be listening well to understand how you can help your buyer achieve his objectives. The most effective way to know when to ask for the sale is by asking "trial closing" questions.

Trial closing questions are open-ended questions meant to determine if you are making progress with your buyer and what objections your buyer has to your recommendations. Think about this situation—you are in a sales conversation and you have been uncovering how you can help your buyer meet his objectives. You have made some preliminary suggestions and you are interested to know if you are making progress in the sales process. This is the time to ask the open-ended trial closing question. You might ask one of the following questions…

1. How do you feel about that?
2. What are your thoughts at this point?
3. What do you think?

These open-ended trial closing questions are meant to elicit a response that lets you know how you are doing. Is your buyer buying into your recommendations? Are you and your buyer seeing eye-to-eye? Does your buyer appear interested in the direction you are taking? If your answers are "yes", then you are making progress toward the sale. If the buyer responds with some kind of objection, then you know how you need to either shift the conversation to something more appealing to the buyer or that you have to overcome that objection. In all cases, you will know what you are dealing with and you should know your next step.

Open-ended trial closing questions are the salesperson's most effective tool because the answers help you chart a course for the rest of the sales conversation. They tell if and when the time is right to ask for the sale.

You have asked open-ended trial closing questions throughout your sales conversation. You have overcome all objections. The buyer seems to agree that your recommendations can support achieving his objectives. Everything you are seeing and hearing from your customer says *"he's ready to buy"*. It's time to ask for the sale.

Sales training programs suggest all kinds of ways to ask for the sale from the "assumptive close" to the "puppy dog close". Personally, I don't like to play games and manipulate anyone, especially someone with whom I'm interested in doing business. So I suggest an approach that is much more straightforward.

When asking for the sale, most of the time you will ask a closed-ended question because you are seeking a "yes" or "no" answer—hopefully a "yes" one. In other cases, your question may not be a "yes or no" question but one in which you offer choices. As such, here are some good questions when asking for the sale…

1. Which of these 3 options would you like to go with?
2. Based on our schedule, we can get started next week. Would you like us to schedule it?
3. Would you prefer the lease or purchase option?
4. If I can meet that time frame, would you like to get things started?
5. We're confident we can achieve your objectives. Would you like to get started?

I don't think there are many salespeople that would be uncomfortable, feel like they are being disrespectful, or think they are coming off like a "snake oil salesman" by asking for the sale using these questions.

In summary, ask open-ended trial closing questions to make sure you are connecting with your buyer and determine when the buyer is ready for you to ask for the sale. Listen intently and overcome any objections. Use closed-ended or choice-type questions when you ask for the sale.

CLOSING RATIO IMPROVEMENT: THE ZOPA TECHNIQUE

As a sales professional, your role is to identify the best solutions, maximize profitable sales for your company, and create raving fans of your customers. This article is about maximizing profitable sales and achieving a 100% close ratio—you read that right—100% close ratio of qualified customers.

Maximizing the size of your average sale depends on several things...

1. Qualify your customer—The BARTS method for qualifying customers. More on the BARTS method in the Prospecting chapter.
2. Ask good questions and listen—This is the only way you can learn how to add value for your customer and ultimately become a trusted advisor.
3. Present options—Give your customers options that increase the probability of making the sale.

One of the principles I learned from my sales experience is called ZOPA—Zone of Possible Agreement. ZOPA is more widely known as a negotiating technique. However, it has become one of the most effective

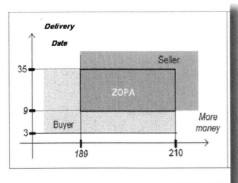

sales principles I have practiced and has increased the average size of a sale by at least 60%. Here's how it works...

Through your conversations with your customer, you identify the best solutions that will achieve the customer's objectives. You also attempt to understand the customer's budget. This is sometimes difficult but through a series of questions and techniques, you can usually gain a pretty good sense of your customer's budget.

Upon identifying the best solutions for your customer and understanding their budget, you create some options. Remember, people like to buy—they don't like to be sold. Instead of putting your customer in a situation where they have to give you a "yes" or "no" to a single solution, offer your customer some options. For simplicity, we will call these options Good—Better—Best. These three options are described as follows...

Good –The lowest priced solution that will work for your customer; priced in a way that virtually guarantees you will close the sale.

Better—An added value solution that will work for your customer, priced at around 60% of the difference between your Good option and your Best option.

Best—The "fully loaded" solution that will get great results for your customer; priced at the very top of your customer's budget range.

Now ask yourself; if you were the customer and someone presented three options that all seemed to make sense and were all priced within your budget range, you'd be more inclined to say "yes" to one of them. That is how you get to 100% close ratio. In support of this, the following graph shows that buyers prefer choices:

When given a proposal, would you rather be presented with... (select one)

Answer	0%	100%	Number of Response(s)	Response Ratio
3 different options that all make sense and priced at different levels like a Good-Better-Best			58	54.2 %
2 different options that all make sense and priced at different levels like Good and Better plans			32	29.9 %
1 solution that appears to make the most sense			17	15.8 %
No Response(s)			0	0.0 %
		Totals	107	100%

In my experience, the customer almost always chooses the Better or the Best option which increases your average sale size.

In summary, listen to your customer, identify solutions that will work for them, become a trusted advisor, and integrate the ZOPA technique into your sales presentations. Your closing ratio and the size of your average sale will increase.

CUSTOMER FRIENDLY CLOSING TECHNIQUES

When you are in a selling situation, it's often uncomfortable to ask for the sale—it just doesn't feel right and makes you feel like just another pushy salesperson.

Studies by sales organizations have consistently identified closing the sale as the single most challenging aspect to implement. When salespeople are observed in live situations, studies found that nearly half of sales calls end without an attempt to close the deal. Additionally, another study found that the national sales closing rate is only about 27%. Yikes!

WHAT IS THE DISCOMFORT IN ASKING FOR THE SALE?

If you have participated in a sales training class, you were probably exposed to several "closing techniques". These are techniques used by salespeople to get a "yes" even though you may not be totally comfortable. Here are some examples of "closing techniques"—some you may have experienced first-hand:

- Alternative close – "would you like to purchase 2 items or 3?"
- Urgency close – "if you buy today, we can take 5% off the price."
- Competitive threat – "we can only sell this to one competitor and if you don't buy it then your competitor may."

When you hear things like this, there's little wonder why salespeople get a bad rap. Statements and questions like these put pressure on the customer to decide. Consequently, many salespeople feel discomfort in using them but, they are appropriate in certain circumstances...

WHEN SHOULD YOU USE CLOSING TECHNIQUES?

Studies found there's an inverse correlation between the price of the sale and the use of closing techniques—the bigger the sale, the fewer closing techniques you should use. Following are a couple of examples...

- You are in a store looking at dress shirts that cost $40 each. The salesperson asks, "Would you like to buy that in blue or yellow or both?" (Alternative close). This question doesn't give you much discomfort because there's little at stake. $40 is $40 but it won't change most people's lives.

- You are shopping for a children's game that costs $70. The salesperson states, "We are running a promotion and if you buy today you will get a $5 gift card toward a future purchase. Would you like to get it today?" (Urgency close). In this situation you might very well thank the salesperson rather than be put off by the pressure to buy.

In smaller sales situations, studies have found the use of closing techniques have at least a neutral effect on closing rates and often, a positive effect.

WHEN SHOULD YOU NOT USE CLOSING TECHNIQUES?
The bigger the sale the less you want to use closing techniques. If your buyer is considering a $5,000 investment and you "pressure" him into making a decision by a certain date, the buyer may well consider your "urgent close" attempt to be pushy and manipulative. This may tarnish your reputation.

If you have done your job well, uncovered problems you can solve, presented solutions that make sense, responded to objections, and answered all the customer's questions, your customer may have sold himself. If you pressure him to make a decision by using a closing technique then you may put the sale at risk. On the other hand, you don't want to leave this discussion dangling or wonder what will happen next. In other words, ask for the sale, but be sure that you do it right.

HOW TO ASK FOR THE BIGGER SALE?
You are at the end of the sales process with a qualified prospect considering a large purchase and it is time to ask for the sale. What is a good way to do it without appearing pushing or manipulative? Here are good questions to ask for the sale…

- Based on our schedule, we can get started next week. Would you like us to schedule it?
- If we can meet your timing requirements, would you like to get things started?
- We're confident we can achieve your objectives. Would you like to get started?
- How would you like things to proceed from here?
- What would you like the next step to be?

It's doubtful that a salesperson would feel pushy or uncomfortable asking any of these questions.

In summary, the larger the sale the less you want to use closing techniques when asking for the sale. When the stakes (and dollars) are high, pressuring the customer to make a decision before he's comfortable can jeopardize your reputation and the sales opportunity. Always ask for the sale, but do so in an honest, straightforward way. You will stand a better chance of closing the deal.

CLOSING THE SALE—THE TOUGHEST PART OF SALES

Some sources say there are over 12 million people in sales positions across the US. Unfortunately, only about 10% of them are successful. The successful ones follow a sales system and know how to ask for the sale. This article is about asking for the sale and includes several effective closing statements that you can incorporate easily into your sales activities.

BE A TRUSTED ADVISOR – NOT A CLOSING MERCENARY

To many, the phrase "closing the sale" has mercenary implications—you are persuading someone to do something they wouldn't normally do. That is never good. Instead of "closing the sale", I prefer to call it "beginning a relationship". I say this because no one wants to be sold. People want to buy and it is the role of the salesperson to ensure the legitimate needs of the customer will be satisfied by the products and services you offer. A good relationship paired with products and services that work for your customer are the two main ingredients to becoming a "trusted advisor". "Trusted advisor" status is what a professional salesperson should always strive for. Enough philosophy—now let's talk about how to make sure you are dealing with a qualified prospect.

QUALIFYING YOUR PROSPECT

Let's face it - if your prospect doesn't meet your qualifications as a real prospect, closing a sale will be hard. Before we talk about closing a sale, I want to share my process for qualifying a prospect. I use the BARTS method—one that I created. A prospect has to meet the BARTS criteria before I invest time to present solutions and close a sale. Here's what B-A-R-T-S means:

B—Does my prospect have the **B**udget to purchase my solution?
A—Does the person I am talking to have the **A**uthority to make a decision?
R—Will the **R**evenue (or profits) I generate from the sale meet my expectations?
T—Is the **T**iming right for the customer to implement my solutions?
S—Do my products/services **S**olve the needs of the prospect?

You may have a different qualifications process and if it works, great! Just make sure you have a solid method to qualify your prospects. If you don't then you may be chasing the wrong people to make a sale. More on the BARTS method in the Prospecting chapter.

SALES ARE MADE BEFORE YOU ASK FOR THE SALE

Becoming a trusted advisor is key to sales success—always be on a path that leads you to becoming a trusted advisor to your customers. Trustworthy relationships built on mutual respect are required in order to become a trusted advisor. Since purchase decisions are primarily emotional then justified with facts, it is critical to develop good rapport and a good relationship with your prospect.

If you have done the following things…

- You have qualified your prospect.
- You have built good rapport and are developing a relationship with your prospect that is trustworthy and based on mutual respect.
- The prospect has agreed to make a decision once everything is discussed…I will think about it" is not a decision. We want a "yes" or "no" at the end.
- You are following a sales system that works for you.
- You have asked good questions and listened well to learn about the prospect.
- You have done a great job of using Trial Closing techniques

…the sale should already be made—at least mentally. You just need to ask for it. So, let's talk about how to close a sale.

CLOSING TECHNIQUES

We are all different and our individual differences are what makes our lives interesting, inspiring, and also what makes the world go around. In sales, we need to understand the unique personalities of prospects in order to ask for the sale in the right way.

The DISC personality assessment instrument is one that we often use in our sales training activities. It is fairly accurate at assessing people and interpretation of the information is not overly complex. If you want to know your DISC profile, there are free online assessments.

The DISC profile reveals personality traits in people that tend to manifest themselves in day-to-day activities, communication styles, and decision-making. DISC has four primary personality types and based on the personality types, I have suggested some good closing questions.

DISC Personality Preference	DISC Personality Attributes	How to Ask for the Sale
Dominant Type	Competitive, goal oriented, wants authority, self-sufficient	"I'm confident this is the plan that will achieve your goals. How would you like to move forward from here?"
Influencer Type	Extroverted, outgoing, builds relationships, socially skilled	"I feel we've built a good relationship and I understand your goals. What would you want the next step to be from here?"
Steady Relater Type	Patient, calm, controlled, willing to help others who they consider "friends"	"I feel this solution is something that will work and is mutually beneficial to both of us. Where would you like to take this from here?"
Compliant Type	Cautious, adaptable, risk averse, orderly, methodical, follows process and procedures	"Well we've gone through the details and I believe this is the most certain solution. What is the next step in the process from your point of view?"

These suggested closing questions all have the following important attributes...

- They are all open-ended questions.
- They all appeal to the unique personality types of the prospect.
- None of them is a "hard close" question or one that would make the normal prospect and salesperson uncomfortable.

Asking for the sale is not hard to do as long as you have built rapport, done a good job asking questions and listening, and have offered solutions that solve the prospect's needs and wants. It is important to qualify your prospect—otherwise you might be trying to close a sale with the wrong person or under less than optimal circumstances. Finally, assess your prospect's personality and ask for the sale in a way he/she can relate. Follow these methods and you will increase your closing performance.

Eight

Following Up on Open Proposals

History proves that one of the leading reasons for lack of sales is poor follow-up on the part of the salesperson.

5 WAYS TO FOLLOW UP WITH BUYERS

Have you ever presented a proposal to a buyer and never gotten a response? The old saying, "love me, hate me, just don't be indifferent to me" is the way I think about these situations. Just tell me something! What are the best tactics to apply when you are in situation like this? This article provides 5 ways to follow up on sales proposals you have presented.

Our research suggests some strategies about how to follow up – see the following charts

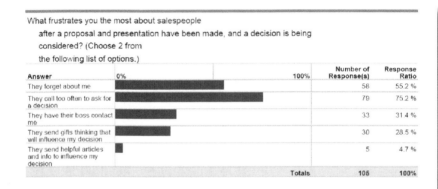

What frustrates you the most about salespeople after a proposal and presentation have been made, and a decision is being considered? (Choose 2 from the following list of options.)			Number of Response(s)	Response Ratio
Answer	0%	100%		
They forget about me			58	55.2 %
They call too often to ask for a decision			79	75.2 %
They have their boss contact me			33	31.4 %
They send gifts thinking that will influence my decision			30	28.5 %
They send helpful articles and info to influence my decision			5	4.7 %
		Totals	**105**	**100%**

What is the best way for a salesperson to follow up (after a sales meeting) on a customer who is considering his/her proposal?			Number of Response(s)	Response Ratio
Answer	0%	100%		
Send email summarizing items covered in meeting			79	73.8 %
Call me and ask for a decision			8	7.4 %
Send some type of greeting card, note or other message just to say top-of-mind			16	14.9 %
Stop by my office to give me a valuable article, additional information, etc.			4	3.7 %
No Response(s)			0	0.0 %
		Totals	**107**	**100%**

1. SET AN EXPECTATION WITH THE BUYER

You have presented your proposal, handled objections, and asked for the sale. They buyer responds "let me think about it" or "I need to talk to my partner about it". Many buyers don't like to make decisions on the spot or under pressure, so don't be disappointed. However, you have done a lot of work and you deserve to know when and how the buyer will make a decision. It is okay for you to ask. Here are some good questions to ask that will help you set an expectation...

> *"I can appreciate your wanting to think about this—when can I expect to hear back from you about a decision?"*
> *"I want to make sure you have all the information you need to make the right decision for you—what criteria will you apply to make a decision?"*

Both of these questions will help you get a commitment from the buyer but don't be shocked if that commitment isn't ultimately met. When it isn't met, apply some of the tactics described below...

2. REINFORCE THE VALUE AND BENEFITS

There are reasons why your solution is valuable to the buyer. When you follow up for a decision, focus on how it will benefit the buyer. Say something like...

> *"You mentioned in our previous meeting how important it was to get sales in the New Year off to a positive start. How about we get back together and establish a plan for moving forward on the proposal to support your sales plan?"*

3. REFERENCE OTHER SUCCESSES

In the B2B selling space, buyers want to know that you understand their business. Sharing real world examples of how you have made a positive impact on similar firms is a great way for buyers to gain credibility and confidence in your product/service. You might say something like...

> *"I was thinking about the importance you place on increasing sales and it reminded me of the work we did with XYZ Company.*

In their case, we implemented many of the things we are suggesting for you and were able to generate many qualified sales leads. Do you have a few minutes for me to explain how that worked for them?"

4. ENHANCE VALUE THROUGH EDUCATION

Buyers are not always in the buying mode, even if they're entertaining a specific proposal you have provided to them. However, they are interested to some degree, or they wouldn't have invested their time with you. So, how do you keep in touch with them without appearing to be a pest? You educate them with valuable information.

Occasionally sending or dropping off an article or report is always a good way to follow up. It shows you are interested and you want to add value to the buyer. You might say something like...

"I was thinking about the solutions we've recommended to you and I came across this article (or report) that talks about business trends in the marketplace. Hope you get some benefit from it. By the way, what are your thoughts about the proposal I shared with you?"

5. IT IS OK TO SAY "NO"

You have done your best job at following up and still no decision. It may be time to ask if the decision is "no". You might say something like...

"It has been a few weeks since I shared our recommendations with you. If you have decided to work with another firm, that is ok. I'd rather know your decision than be left wondering. Please let me know if you have decided to work with someone else. If you haven't, perhaps we should get back together to review how our plan will achieve your objectives."

When following up with buyers, it's not just about poking around for a decision, it's about adding value. The buyer may be interested and may have asked you to check back in with them, but don't be like every other average salesperson. Raise your game to the next level by providing value in every interaction with a buyer. Do this and you will get more "yes" decisions to your proposals.

MANAGING YOUR SALES FUNNEL

People don't like to be sold—they do like to buy. Consequently, I never recommend selling something to someone who either doesn't need it or won't get value from it.

One of my theories about selling is this—someone sells something when the **need intersects with awareness**. That is, when the need develops and the prospect is aware that your product or service might satisfy that need, you have a chance to make a sale. Conversely, if there is no legitimate need, and your prospect is not aware of your product or service, then there is no sale.

One of the most important elements in sales is managing your "sales funnel" so that when the prospect's need does arise, he/she is aware of your product or service and a conversation can ensue.

As I mentioned before, if it's not the right time, you won't make the sale. Generally, you can't control the prospect's timing. You can only control the extent to which he/she is aware of your product or service. This is why managing your sales funnel is extremely important.

Some guidelines for managing your sales funnel…

1. Only qualified prospects should be in your funnel. Each prospect may not meet all the BARTS criteria, but if you believe at some point they might, they belong in your funnel.
2. Assess each prospect with an A, B, C or D based on when you think the right time will be. "A" prospects will likely purchase within 30 days, "B" prospects within 90 days, and "C" prospects within 6 months and "D" prospects sometime beyond 6 months. These times may vary based on the nature of your product or service. What is important is that you categorize your prospects based on timing.
3. Include pertinent information about the prospect, like type of business, previous interactions, appropriate products/services, etc. A good Customer Relationship Management (CRM) system like Salesforce, ACT or others may be appropriate.
4. Document every interaction you have with each prospect in your funnel.

Now that you have a solid sales funnel, full of qualified prospects, how do you make sure they are always aware of you so that when the need arises, you are there? Here are some guidelines for managing awareness with your sales funnel...

- Email marketing is a great way to stay in front of your prospects. If you do email marketing, don't send junk. Send something of value that doesn't take a lot of time to consume. A monthly email is recommended.
- For "A" prospects, "touch" them once a week. After all, they are ready to buy within 30 days so you want to stay top-of-mind.
- For "B" prospects, "touch" them once every 2-4 weeks.
- For "C" prospects, "touch" them once every 4-6 weeks.
- For "D" prospects, use your email marketing campaign to stay in touch.

WHAT IS A "TOUCH"?

"Touches" represent any type of interaction with a prospect. It could be an email, a phone call, a written note, a stop-in to say hello, an article, etc. Make sure that your "touches" add value. Don't just call up and say "are you ready to buy yet?" A better call could be "I thought about (one of your objections) and figured a way to solve it." I often send articles that are pertinent to the business or to a personal interest of the prospect. Whatever you do, be credible and don't waste the prospect's time.

In summary, record every meaningful interaction with a potential prospect in your sales funnel. Rate each one based on when you think he/she will be ready to buy. Based on timing, "touch" them with value added interactions. Do this, and no doubt your sales will greatly increase.

Nine

Sales Training

You might have the DNA to be an elite salesperson, but if you don't have the skills, your performance will be marginalized.

WHY CUSTOMIZED SALES TRAINING IS THE BETTER CHOICE

Sales training without customized skill practice and ongoing follow up is like getting your knee replaced and ignoring post-surgery physical therapy. It is never quite the same. We've all experienced it before—well maybe not the knee surgery part. You attend a one or two-day sales training seminar and at the end, you feel like you can conquer the world. You feel like a selling beast. In the training and development industry, we call this feeling the "post training high".

Sales training and skill development are great things, and they work. A recent study, by a reputable research firm, reported that sales training programs which include post-training reinforcement, achieve a meaningful improvement in year-over-year sales. This compares to an actual decline in year-over-year sales when no reinforcement is applied. Additionally, participants involved in sales training programs that included post-training reinforcement, experienced a 10%+ gain in sales quota attainment and customer renewal rates.

How do you ensure your time and money investments in sales training pay off? This article provides 3 strategies for getting the most from your sales training investments.

CUSTOMIZED SKILLS TRAINING

There are a finite number of core selling principles that are part of most sales training seminars. Getting exposure to these principles will likely create behavior changes at least for a short period of time. When core principles can be customized for a particular firm's sales environment and process, the impact on actual sales performance increases dramatically.

Taking these basic selling principles and molding them to be applied in a specific sales environment is key. Creating customized sales training will take the salespersons performance to a whole new level. For example, we provide sales training to a local fitness organization. Developing and training people on prospecting behaviors right there on the gym floor is far more effective than it would be if we were just talking about them conceptually in a classroom. That is customized skills training.

ROLE PLAYS & SKILL PRACTICE

You know what they say "practice makes perfect". However, you don't necessarily want your salespeople just practicing on live subjects—your buyers. Instead, set up an environment in which you frequently conduct skill practice sessions where salespeople can practice executing the main sales principles.

Role plays are best done with 3 people; the salesperson, someone playing the buyer role, and an observer. The observer is an important role because the salesperson and the person acting as the buyer are caught up in the transaction and are unable to make specific notes about what occurred during the skill practice. On the contrary, the observer is a neutral third party able to take notes about what the salesperson actually said and how he performed.

VIDEOTAPING & CALL RECORDING

The ultimate in sales training skill practice is recording the interaction. In situations where the salesperson and buyer are face-to-face, videotaped role playing is best. In situations where the sales transaction is done over the phone, call recording is the way to go.

If you have never used this skill practice technique before, I'd encourage you to try it—the results are amazing! Conducting a recorded role play enables you to hear word-for-word what was said, and see how the buyer reacted to the salesperson. The best part is that the salesperson is able to critique themselves. What better way to learn than to identify on your own, what you could have done differently?

We provide sales development training for a local lawn care company and have used this technique consistently. The first couple of sessions were a little intimidating to the participants but after a few times, they quickly got used to the idea and now embrace it as a great way to learn, help each other out, and develop their ability to execute the main selling principles.

In summary, if you are sending your salespeople to sales training seminars then you are to be congratulated for taking that first step. However, if there is no customization or follow up skill development, you are likely finding that your sales team is not improving from the sales training investments you have made.

Creating a development environment in which the selling skills your team has learned are customized to fit your particular selling environment, is the first step to achieving a payback from your training dollars. Doing frequent roles plays to practice the selling skills and recording those skill practices will cause behaviors to actually change. That is when you start to see meaningful improvements in the performance of your salespeople.

HOW SALES TRAINING GENERATES AN ROI

Is it really worth investing in sales assessment tools and sales training? The Aberdeen Group, a leading national research firm, conducted a study of more than 800 end-user companies about their activities and investments in sales assessments and sales training. They compared the actual sales results in relation to the companies' investments in a variety of sales related activities. This article is a synopsis of the results of this research study.

ASSESSMENTS OF SALES PERSONNEL

In relation to the impact of doing pre-employment and incumbent selling skills assessments, the Aberdeen study evaluated four dimensions; 1) attainment of the sales team quota, 2) customer retention, 3) individual sales rep quota attainment and 4) quota attainment of new sales reps.

Companies that invested in sales assessments saw their overall quota attainment and customer retention levels perform about 10% better than those firms that didn't use assessments tools. Also, in relation to individual performance and performance of new reps, firms investing in sales assessments were 30-40% more successful.

METHODS USED TO TRAIN SALES PERSONNEL

What is the most effective way to train sales personnel—classroom, OJT, mentoring, etc.? The Aberdeen Study evaluated the sales performance of companies comparing their approach to sales training against their sales performance.

Instructor-led sales training is by far the most popular and effective approach. 83% of the top performing companies and 75% of all companies in the study reported using this method of training—more than twice the frequency of any other approach.

POST INSTRUCTOR LED TRAINING & COACHING

Anyone with good experience in the training and development business understands that behavior doesn't change much unless there's an ongoing investment in practice, coaching, behavior reinforcement, and evaluation. We often call it the "feel good syndrome". You participate in class-room training and when it's done, you feel like you can conquer the world. You get back to work and "reality" sets in. If you are not organized and committed to implement at least some of the behaviors and practices from the training class, no real behavior change occurs.

The Aberdeen Study charted sales performance against post-training activities and found a meaningful difference in the companies who invested in post-training activities compared to those who did not.

Interestingly, post training reinforcement had the biggest impact on overall team performance and speed with which newer people achieved high productivity levels. This implies that post-training reinforcement impacts teamwork among a sales team.

The Aberdeen Study leaves little mystery about the impact of sales assessments. Furthermore, the study reinforces the popularity and impact of instructor-led sales training and post-training reinforcement activities.

In summary, if you want to increase revenue through a highly effective sales force, invest in pre-employment sales assessments, use sales assessments tools to identify strengths and areas of development among your current sales personnel, and invest in instructor-led sales training and post-training reinforcement.

THE 4 BEST-SELLING SKILLS I HAVE PAID TO LEARN

If you are in the role of salesperson yourself or you are footing the bill for a sales team, how do you know what selling skills training is best? What skills are actually "trainable" and how will your investments in sales training pay off the most?

You certainly don't want to waste your time and money on a course when much of the content may not be applicable to your situation. After all, you don't want to change the individual's personality, but rather equip him/her with some basic selling skills that will increase sales.

When you combine the natural personality of the salesperson with a good sales process, and then arm him/her with the right selling skills, you set yourself up for solid success.

In our experience and based on research data from decision-makers, following are the 4 selling skills that will generate the biggest payoff...

1. HOW TO ASK FOR THE SALE

One study indicated that 73% of the sales opportunities go by without the salesperson asking for the sale. Shameful. How do you ask for the sale? Every situation is different. Don't use the manipulative closing techniques that are suggested by a lot of the sales training courses. See the Closing chapter for more information on good closing techniques.

Salespeople should be trained to hear buying signals and to observe body language that suggests the buyer is ready to make a decision. Also, salespeople should be assisted in developing 2-3 methods that ask the customer to make a decision about next steps. Read more about asking for the sale in the Closing chapter.

2. HOW TO UNCOVER A PROBLEM AND CREATE VALUE

Our research tells us that buyers value a salesperson's problem solving skills. In fact, when we asked what separates a good salesperson from his/her peers, "demonstrates ability to solve my problem" was most important.

In addition, when we asked decision-makers what other traits they value most in salespeople, "actively listens to me" and "asks good questions" came out on top, cited by more than ¾ of the respondents.

When you combining the importance of problem solving skills with questioning and listening skills, it is clear that salespeople should be trained and developed to ask the right questions, listen actively for underlying thoughts and motives, and lead a conversation with a buyer to identify and solve the buyer's problem.

3. HOW TO GAIN CREDIBILITY WITH YOUR BUYER

Many call this building rapport, but I like to think of this as simply gaining credibility with the buyer. No buyer is going to buy from you unless they trust you.

Building rapport and credibility with your buyer comes with a variety of skills in which salespeople should develop. These skills include…

- How to greet the buyer to gain a great first impression.
- How to ask a good opening question to get the conversation going.
- How to read/assess the natural communication style of the buyer.
- How to adjust your communication style to match that of the buyer.

Salespeople who are able to do these things well will quickly generate an emotional connection with the buyer and develop good credibility. More on building credibility in the Rapport chapter.

4. HOW TO TRIAL CLOSE AND OVERCOME OBJECTIONS

One of the greatest skills for any salesperson to develop is how to trial close. There's no way you can understand and solve a buyer's problem if you are not good at asking trial closing questions. Training salespeople on how to trial close will reap huge benefits.

Closely related to trial closing is overcoming objections. Often, when you ask a good trial closing question, the buyer may respond with some kind of objection or question that challenges one element of your offering. Developing a salesperson's ability to acknowledge an objection, be empathetic about it, and make a statement to address it, is paramount to sales success. More on trial closing and overcoming objections in the Questions chapter.

In summary, when it comes to developing yourself as a salesperson or developing a team of salespeople, invest your training dollars in certain skills. Don't try to change the personality of your salesperson or think that you can re-engineer how he/she operates. Instead, focus your development efforts on how to ask questions and listen to identify and solve problems, how to gain credibility with your buyer, how to ask trial closing questions, and how to ask for the sale.

Made in the USA
Columbia, SC
19 June 2018